MAYER CENTER SYMPOSIUM XX | READINGS IN LATIN AMERICAN STUDIES

Neocolonial

Inventing Modern Latin American Nations

JORGE F. RIVAS PÉREZ AND LYNDA KLICH

Published by the Mayer Center
for Ancient and Latin American Art
at the Denver Art Museum

100 W. 14th Ave. Pkwy
Denver, CO 80204
mayercenter.denverartmuseum.org
denverartmuseum.org

The Denver Art Museum is located on the homeland of the Arapaho, Cheyenne, and Ute people, along with many people from other Indigenous nations that call this place home. Learn more about our commitments to better represent, elevate, and support Indigenous cultures and people, past and present, on our website.

ISBN 978-1-945483-15-8

Library of Congress Control Number: 2024939883

Design: Nancy Bratton Design

Managing Editor: Valerie Hellstein

Editor: Leslie Murrell

Printed by D&K Printing, Boulder, CO

Distributed by University of Oklahoma Press, Norman, OK

Front cover: Alfredo Boulton, photograph of El Silencio, ca. 1945. Getty Research Institute. © J. Paul Getty Trust.

Back cover: Alfredo Boulton, photograph of El Silencio, ca. 1945. Getty Research Institute. © J. Paul Getty Trust.

CONTENTS

Foreword

The Denver Art Museum's Latin American art collection, encompassing works from the 1500s to today, is one of the largest and most comprehensive in the United States and one of the best in the world. Beginning in 1936 with a gift of *santos* from Anne Evans, it grew rapidly over the years thanks to generous donors, including the Frank Barrows Freyer Collection, Robert C. Appleman, the Stapleton Foundation of Latin American Colonial Art (made possible by the Renchard family), the Frederick and Jan Mayer Collection, and the Colección Patricia Phelps de Cisneros.

Since 1968, the department has expanded due to the support and enthusiasm of longtime museum trustee Frederick Mayer and his wife, Jan. In 2001, the Mayers endowed the department, allowing not only the growth of the collection but also enhanced and robust programming. This gift made it possible to establish the first curatorial position exclusively dedicated to Spanish colonial Latin American art in the United States.

The Mayers also founded the Frederick and Jan Mayer Center for Ancient and Latin American Art at the Denver Art Museum, dedicated to increasing awareness and promoting scholarship in these fields. The endowment sponsors academic activities, including annual symposia, fellowships, study trips, conservation, research projects, and publications. Since 2001, the Mayer Center has held a symposium nearly every year.

My gratitude goes to Jorge F. Rivas Pérez, Frederick and Jan Mayer Curator of Latin American Art, and Lynda Klich, Associate Professor at Hunter College, CUNY, in New York, for their dedication in organizing the 2022 symposium. Scholars from Latin America and the United States spent the day exploring how artists and intellectuals in newly created democratic nations turned to the visual regime of imperial Spain for new inspiration at a time of rising consciousness of the centrality of Indigenous cultures and Panamericanism. The resulting Neocolonial style encompassed myriad contradictions that can still be felt in many Latin American countries today. The papers delivered on November 5, 2022, comprise this volume.

For the past fifty years, the Mayers have generously supported the museum's larger mission. Though Frederick left us far too soon in 2007, Jan has continued his spirit of generosity and enthusiasm for the museum. We offer our thanks to her for her ongoing dedication to the museum as a whole and to the study of ancient and Latin American art in particular.

Christoph Heinrich
Frederick and Jan Mayer Director
Denver Art Museum

Fig. 1. José Clemente Orozco, *Via Crucis* (Christ Carrying the Cross), ca. 1940. Gouache on canvas, 33⅝ × 29½ in. Denver Art Museum: Gift of Nancy Rogers and Edward D. Pierson in memory of Mary Vandusen and Charles Bolles-Rogers, 1983.241.

JORGE F. RIVAS PÉREZ AND LYNDA KLICH

Introduction

In the first half of the 1900s, Latin American artists, architects, and designers searched for visual languages that matched the modern identities of their young nations. Surprisingly, many found their answers in the aesthetics of their colonial past. This book explores the paradoxical nature of the Neocolonial style by examining a wide array of art, from painting and architecture to furniture and graphic design. A group of international scholars probes the meanings, cultural agendas, and contradictions that emerged when artists in democratic nations grounded their work in the visual regime of imperial Spain at a time of rising consciousness of Indigenous cultures and Panamericanism. Facing the mandates and challenges of modernization and a changing global order, artists and intellectuals throughout the Western hemisphere harnessed the power of a shared history that harked back centuries. The lettered class—government officials, intellectuals, theorists, architects, and artists—who drove cultural production in Latin America deployed this history and its referents for various reasons. They were responding to nineteenth- and twentieth-century regimes on both ends of the political spectrum—including influential periods of liberalism in Argentina and the coercive dictatorships of Porfirio Díaz in Mexico and Juan Vicente Gómez in Venezuela. The colonial was harnessed to advance or counter modernizing ideas and, ironically, to mark centennials of Independence from Spain. In this era of national consciousness, moreover, the rich and malleable history of the Neocolonial style allowed for the construction of identities that at once distinguished modern Latin American nations globally, because of its emphasis on *mestizaje* (defined then as the mixing of Spanish and Indigenous heritages), and as anti-Anglo, united against the increasing global influence of the United States.

Several works in the Denver Art Museum's collection embody both the prevalence and the contradictions of the Neocolonial and confirm the style's efficacy as ideologically potent, including *Via Crucis* (Christ Carrying the Cross, ca. 1940), commissioned from the Mexican muralist José Clemente Orozco (1883–1949) by Charles Bolles Bolles-Rogers, a business executive and collector (fig.1).[1] The work exhibits the artist's trademark expressionist style, with strong diagonal brushstrokes, raw, earthy colors enlivened strategically with areas of brighter color, and exaggerated figuration. Its subject matter of Christ on the road to Calvary speaks to Orozco's summoning of fatalistic heroes, such as the Mesoamerican god Quetzalcoatl and the Greek god Prometheus, who sacrificed themselves for the sake of history. The prominence of Christian themes in his work conforms to his acerbic vision of history as a repeating cycle of creation and destruction, which played into the staunchly anti-Catholic intellectual environment of postrevolutionary Mexico, especially among his radically leftist artist colleagues. *Via Crucis*, in one sense, recalls Orozco's later recollection that iconographical elements familiar from colonial-era religious painting appeared in "revolutionary socialist propaganda . . . with surprising consistency."[2] In other works by Orozco, and those by other muralists, Christ transforms into a fallen soldier or subjugated worker, halos appear as sombreros, the Virgin's mantle as a rebozo, and the cross as a barricade. Nonetheless, the colonial sources underneath these compositions remain unmistakable. As Orozco's own words suggest, many of these works aimed to ennoble rural and urban Indigenous and mestizo workers and revolutionaries, using a familiar visual language to soften the blow of social change for the elite. Orozco's *Via Crucis* confirms the continued power of such motifs to generate emotion while speaking to entrenched structures of colonialist authority, relating to the connections he made between Christ and the conquistador Hernán Cortes in his mural cycles at Dartmouth College in New Hampshire (1932–34) and the Hospicio Cabañas in Guadalajara (1937–39).

The cover made by Francisco Díaz de León (1897–1975) for Mariano Silva y Aceves's 1925 *Campanitas de Plata* (Little silver bells), in turn, is an example of the use of the diffusion of the

Fig. 2. Francisco Díaz de León, "Campanitas de plata, libro de niños. 54 maderas originales de Diaz de León" (Little silver bells, children's storybook. 54 original woodcut prints by Díaz de León), title page in *Campanitas de plata: libro de niños* by Mariano Silva y Aceves (Mexico: Editorial Cultura, 1925). Woodcut print on cardboard paper, 7⅞ × 6¾ in. Denver Art Museum Library Rare Books Collection, 00045796.

Fig. 3. Francisco Díaz de León, "La fuente a media noche" (The Fountain at Midnight). In *Campanitas de plata: libro de niños* by Mariano Silva y Aceves (Mexico: Editorial Cultura, 1925), 55. Woodblock print on paper, 4⅝ × 4⅝ in. Denver Art Museum Library Rare Books Collection, 00045796.

Neocolonial into daily life and educational practices in postrevolutionary Mexico (fig. 2). A children's book, *Campanitas de Plata* contained fifty-four woodcuts by Díaz de León that framed Silva y Aceves's brief novel with ornamented initial capitals and calm scenes with fountains, arched doorways, and aqueducts that evoke *los días de antaño*, or the days of yesteryear, frequently recalled with a falsely uncomplicated nostalgia by colonial chroniclers in the early twentieth century (fig. 3). But these placid scenes had ulterior motives. *Capanitas de Plata* was published by Editorial Cultura, a leading organization in a widespread push to spread literacy among the uneducated populous of Indigenous and mestizo working classes in postrevolutionary Mexico. Although Cultura's portfolio varied, many educational endeavors, including those pioneered by the Mexican government, emphasized Spanish-language classics—and a visual style that matched New Spanish book production, suggesting the Peninsular as the literary paradigm—that is, the language of the cultivated. This process not only valued Spanish heritage but also elided Indigenous cultural practices such as oral histories.

Beyond painting, sculpture, and the graphic arts, starting in the late nineteenth century and gaining momentum into the twentieth century, there was a growing public interest in the material culture from the colonial era, particularly furniture and ceramics. The first studies on Spanish colonial material culture emerged around this time, with authors such as Manuel Romero de Terreros in Mexico, Alfredo Taullard in Argentina, and Arístides Rojas in Venezuela paving the way with their notable publications.[3] These studies served as guiding lights, inspiring subsequent generations of architects, designers, and artists to create neocolonial designs for the home.

Fig. 4. Unknown artist, *Side Chair*, ca. 1930–40. Wood with fabric upholstery, 47 × 21¼ × 19¼ in. Denver Art Museum: Gift of Robert J. Stroessner, 1991.1155.

Neocolonial furnishings, while drawing inspiration from the past, are not mere replicas. Designers of this era often used historical pieces as a starting point, incorporating traditional ornamental styles and frequently employing artisanal production methods. However, the resulting pieces diverged from historical originals. Designers made significant adjustments in proportions and scale to adapt to the needs of modern life and the architecture of the time. Neocolonial buildings have more modest dimensions when compared to the grandeur of the Hispanic period.

Incorporating ornamental repertoires mixed with modern motifs tailored to the preferences of contemporary consumers was a common practice. For instance, a side chair in the museum's collection is a prime example of this type of adaptation (fig. 4). While it may initially resemble a Mexican chair from the second half of the eighteenth century, closer examination reveals its stylized, elongated proportions and other subtle changes. The exaggerated curves of the legs and deep undulations of the front and side seat rails create a more dramatic effect if compared to historical chairs. Additionally, the deeper and bolder carvings add to its modern appeal. The production of such furniture blends machinery with handcrafted techniques.

Another example in the collection is a glazed earthenware plate from Michoacán, likely from the 1920s or early 1930s (fig. 5). This piece adheres to a centuries-old tradition of Mexican tin-glazed ceramics in its materials and manufacturing. However, its elegant yet simple decoration featuring birds in flight in green and orange enamel and blue leafy details reflects a modern taste. Undoubtedly, this plate was crafted with a more contemporary clientele in mind.

This fusion of old and new found in all types of furniture and home goods appealed to consumers with more traditional tastes. These designs, in one way or another, struck a chord of familiarity with the general public while representing the latest and most fashionable styles of the time. Moreover, these objects carried significant connotations of social class and purchasing power.

For the bourgeoisie and political elites, there was a deep appreciation for a sense of historical continuity and a direct link to the splendor and refined taste of the Spanish era. These groups saw neocolonial-style objects and buildings as a reflection of their status and embraced them as symbols of their social standing. For those aspiring to ascend the social ladder, this connection with history legitimized their newfound position in society. It aligned their tastes with those of the wealthy and provided a tangible link to a bygone era of opulence and sophistication.

The essays in this book confront head on the various contradictions around the Neocolonial, especially its status as an art form that, while looking back at centuries-old visual traditions, was situated by its practitioners as decidedly modern, whether in its materials, purposes, or ideological foundations or in its engagement with new phenomena such as tourism, automobile culture, and progressive education ideals.

In "Neocolonial Architecture for a Modern Capital: Carlos Raúl Villanueva's Urban Renewal of El Silencio in Caracas (1942–45)," Jorge F. Rivas Pérez explores the first important urban housing project in mid-century Venezuela, which contained apartments, commercial spaces, fountains, and gardens, that replaced a blighted neighborhood filled with narrow streets and crumbling buildings. Situating Villanueva's planned "city within a city" within Venezuelan architectural history, as well as within Villanueva's own oeuvre, Rivas

Pérez reveals how the project modeled how city planners and ideologues used the Neocolonial to mark the modern city with spaces that engaged with then-circulating racial theories, in this case, Alfredo Boulton's *belleza criolla.*

In her essay, "Casa Zuno: Revolutionary *Gesamtkunstwerk,*" Lynda Klich analyzes one of the more remarkable private residences from postrevolutionary Mexico: the 1923 home of José Guadalupe Zuno Hernández, governor of Jalisco. Klich situates Casa Zuno within the early-1920s cultural, political, and social context of Mexico and Guadalajara, arguing that it embodies the concept of a *Gesamtkunstwerk*, the allover work of art. This residence exemplifies the paradoxes of a transformative era for the nation, a time of new beginnings when dominant social and racial hierarchies aimed to shape an idealized image of the revolutionary Mexican citizen. Casa Zuno served as a canvas for artists, artisans, and designers who sought to forge a national identity by symbolically weaving together Mexico's Indigenous and Spanish cultural heritages into a modern, unified narrative.

Fig. 5. Unknown artist, *Plate*, ca. 1920–30. Ceramic, 2⅜ × 14½ in. dia. Denver Art Museum: Gift of Mr. and Mrs. John Critcher Freyer, 1988.3.

Cristina López Uribe's "Antagonisms: Neocolonial vs. Functionalism in Mexico" explores the conflicting architectural approaches that emerged in Mexico in the 1930s. Against a backdrop of complex cultural influences—local traditions, the growing presence of the United States, and the enduring legacy of Spanish culture—López Uribe examines the efforts to craft a new international image for the nation while forging a distinct Mexican identity. She argues that the rise of the Neocolonial can be partly attributed to the lingering imagery and rhetoric of the Mexican Revolution, alongside idealized notions of rural life that resonated with the revolutionaries' aspirations.

In turn, Horacio Ramos, in "Adobe Modernism: Enrique Camino Brent and Colonial Architecture in Modern Peru," focuses on the artist's use of his own studio in the San Isidro neighborhood of Lima as a site of experimentation. He outlines two essential elements that made Camino Brent's Neocolonial style stand out. First is Camino Brent's insertion of architectural signifiers of the rural—specifically a "muddy" white facade—into the bustling capital city (which he, of course, achieved through the very modern material of concrete). Second is his insistent elevation of Indigenous craft in the building's interior, as well as in his own artistic practice.

In "Aesthetics of Excess: Lima's Neocolonial Imaginary (1870–1950)," Ricardo Kusunoki Rodríguez examines the intellectual debates and ideologies that fueled Peru's embrace of neocolonial visual culture in the 1920s and '30s. He explores how this style shaped national identity and also the modern urban image of the capital city, Lima. Kusunoki Rodríguez analyzes the thinking of figures like José de la Riva Agüero y Osma and Ricardo Palma, highlighting the tension between the physical remnants of the colonial past and the contemporary nationalist aspirations that the Neocolonial was meant to embody.

Carla Guillermina García's essay, "Martín Noel: Cultural Routes and Pictorial Maps," focuses on the leading architect and thinker's lesser-known profile as a cultural promoter through his work for the Argentine National Academy. In seeking to bring his country into the Panamerican dialogue about Hispanic tradition, García shows, Noel concentrated on the country's northwest Andean provinces, which allowed him to connect the region, whose status during the viceroyalty was not significant, to the much more prominent viceroyalty of Peru. García explores Noel's production of maps, pamphlets, and guides to demonstrate his insertion of this colonial past into a very modern network of new roads.

In her contribution, "Neocolonial Design in Mexico, 1940–1970: From a Lost Heritage to a Modern Vocabulary," Ana Elena Mallet delves into the key designers who sought to forge a new aesthetic for modern Mexico. These designers drew inspiration from the country's rich colonial past and its enduring artisanal traditions. Mallet presents how their work emerged from a dynamic exchange of ideas among architects and designers, all vying to define a uniquely Mexican style in a time marked by a vibrant debate between prioritizing functionality over pure aesthetics and reconciling the cosmopolitan spirit of twentieth-century modernism with the enduring appeal of Spanish colonial architecture, a symbol of Mexico's distinct heritage.

Finally, Marina Garone Gravier's text, "The Neocolonial in the History of Books and Publishing in Postrevolutionary Mexico," introduces graphic design inspired by colonial sources as diverse as blacksmithing, ceramics, and lapidary inscriptions that was promoted by four prominent cultural figures, Joaquín García Icazbalceta, Enrique Fernández Ledesma, Justino

Fernández, and Francisco Díaz de León. Through collecting, scholarly publications, and design, these figures, Garone demonstrates, helped build the repertory of neocolonial typography, leaving an understudied, but widespread, stamp on the vast array of production within projects and programs aimed at stemming illiteracy in Mexico.

This book and the Mayer Center symposium that led to it have at their roots a dialogue with the foundational publication on the Neocolonial style in Latin America, *Arquitectura neocolonial: América Latina, Caribe, Estados Unidos* (1994), edited by Aracy A. Amaral.[4] This text brought together experts from throughout the Western hemisphere to examine local and regional manifestations of the Neocolonial. Taken together, these essays also confirm the expansive reach of Neocolonial style in South, Central, and North America, while remaining focused on the built environment, as much scholarship since has done. *Neocolonial: Inventing Modern Latin American Nations* instead reflects recent scholarly developments in the consideration of the colonial revival, specifically by expanding the purview beyond architecture, while acknowledging the fundamental role of architects in advancing this phenomenon. As noted above, the work of the scholars united here brings attention to neocolonial painting, decorative arts, urban planning, graphic design, and tourist endeavors. As well, several of the studies push forward the temporal period of the Neocolonial, examining important neocolonial works that continue through mid-century and beyond. By highlighting diverse locations, media, and sites, *Neocolonial: Inventing Modern Latin American Nations* sheds new light on the contradictions and controversies of the neocolonial endeavor, breaking new paths for the study of this underestimated cultural current.

Notes

1. Bolles-Rogers served in the Red Cross during World War II and later built a varied collection, ranging from Greek terracottas and Byzantine icons to contemporary art. See Laura Jean Louise Sims, "Reflections on a Collection: Revisiting the UWM Icons Fifty Years Later" (master's thesis, University of Wisconsin-Milwaukee, 2015), 22–24, and his obituary, "C. B. Bolles-Rogers," *New York Times*, September 11, 1975, https://www.nytimes.com/1975/09/11/archives/cb-bollesrogers.html.

2. José Clemento Orozco, "Notes Concerning the Technique of Mural Painting in Mexico during the Last Twenty-Five Years," in *¡Orozco! 1883–1949* (Oxford, UK: Museum of Modern Art, 1980), 116. Originally published in 1947.

3. See for example Manuel Romero de Terreros, *Las artes industriales en la Nueva España* (Mexico City: Librería de Pedro Robredo, 1923); Alfredo Taullard, *El mueble colonial sudamericano* (Buenos Aires: Ediciones Peuser, 1947); and Arístides Rojas, *Obras escogidas de Arístides Rojas* (Paris: Garnier Hermanos, 1907).

4. Aracy A. Amaral, *Arquitectura neocolonial: América Latina, Caribe, Estados Unidos* (São Paulo: Memorial; Fondo de Cultura Económica,1994).

JORGE F. RIVAS PÉREZ

Neocolonial Architecture for a Modern Capital: Carlos Raúl Villanueva's Urban Renewal of El Silencio in Caracas (1942–45)

Located in the western part of Caracas, the El Silencio neighborhood is known for its cultural and historical significance. The area is home to several important landmarks, including Plaza O'Leary, buildings by Carlos Raúl Villanueva (1900–1975), and El Calvario park. It is also a popular destination for shopping, dining, and entertainment, with many restaurants, bars, and shops. Starting in the mid-1940s, images of El Silencio printed on postcards have become closely identified with the capital of Venezuela. In this essay, I will examine the contextual background, historical evolution, and significance of both the neighborhood and of the urban renewal plan that reshaped a significant portion of the city in the 1940s, marking the inception of modern Caracas. Additionally, I will delve into the cultural and political milieu of the era, encompassing themes such as nationalism and race, and the concept of *belleza criolla* (creole beauty) coined by the photographer and art patron Alfredo Boulton (1908–1995) in the 1920s.

In colonial times, what is now El Silencio was a poor village west of the Caroata Creek on the outskirts of the city next to a hill named El Calvario (the Calvary; fig. 1). During the pestilence of 1658, mortality was so high that when the *cabildo* sent a commission to check on the village, they recorded what they witnessed: "Only silence, silence, a profound silence," and from that moment, the place was named El Silencio.[1] As happened in other Latin American countries, in Venezuela, the aftermath of the independence wars, roughly spanning from the late 1820s to the 1860s, was a turbulent time of political and economic instability.

The presidencies of Antonio Guzmán Blanco and his allies from 1870 to 1888 bought Venezuela peace, stability, and economic growth. It was also a time of significant urban change and substantial investments in infrastructure. An inveterate Francophile and fervent admirer of Napoleon III , Guzmán Blanco planned a series of projects, inspired by the ideas that Baron Haussmann (1809–1891) had for Paris, in his quest to transform the colonial city—a symbol of the Spanish authority—into a monumental, republican capital. For the president, the architecture of power was that of the authoritarian government of the French Emperor: monumental, ornate, and associated with modernization, cosmopolitanism, and health. The plan for Caracas included significant urban redevelopments around the city center and the construction or renovation of the most important public buildings in the French taste. As part of

Fig. 1. After Joseph Thomas, *View of the City of Caracas from the Calvary*, 1839. Lithograph on paper. Colección Patricia Phelps de Cisneros. Photograph courtesy of Colección Patricia Phelps de Cisneros.

his proposal, in the early 1880s, Guzmán Blanco developed El Calvario hill and the surrounding areas to the west into a park and botanical garden named after himself that opened to the public in 1883. Considered by architectural historian Leszek Zawisza to be the most remarkable public garden from nineteenth-century Venezuela, the park combined ideas borrowed from French and English parks.[2] Despite Guzmán Blanco's grandiose plans for Caracas, the funding available for such a substantial urban overhaul was limited at the time. Next to the newly created park, El Silencio remained part of the colonial city's square grid, characterized by narrow streets and small low buildings, remaining an impoverished and run-down area well into the twentieth century. The city changed very little during the unstable years following the collapse of the Guzmán Blanco regime. The situation did not improve under the long and bloody dictatorship of Juan Vicente Gómez , which lasted from 1908 until his death in December 1935, in part because Gómez disliked the capital city and moved with his entourage to Maracay.

Throughout Latin American nations from the 1860s until the late 1920s, the newly independent countries embarked on modernizations to detach themselves from their Spanish colonial past. Architecture and urbanism from the period were deeply rooted in French models, at the time associated with ideas of modernization and development.[3] In the early 1900s, Caracas architects working in historical styles fashionable at the time, such as Neomoorish and Neogothic, dominated the scene, chief among them Juan Hurtado Manrique (1837–1896) and Alejandro Chataing (1873–1928). Although by the 1930s, we see some openings toward a modernist approach in the works of a younger generation of architects, such as Carlos Guinand (1889–1963) and Gustavo

Wallis Legórburu (1897–1979), historical styles were still favored for grand public buildings.

The Neocolonial Style in Venezuela

In October 1927, Manuel Mujica Millán (1897–1963), a young Spanish architect trained in Barcelona, arrived in Venezuela.[4] He was hired to oversee the construction of the Beaux Arts Majestic Hotel, the most ambitious building in 1920s Caracas. Mujica Millán's successful completion of the building opened the door to new projects in Venezuela, chief among them the renovation of the National Pantheon of Venezuela in Caracas, a mausoleum for Simón Bolívar and other national heroes. By an 1874 decree by President Guzmán Blanco, the 1783 colonial church of the Holy Trinity was converted to the National Pantheon to become the resting place for the remains of the founding father of the homeland. At that time, the church was enlarged and renovated in the Neogothic style by José Gregorio Solano (1810–1879).[5] In 1911, Alejandro Chataing did another renovation preserving the Neogothic style proposed by Solano.[6] However, in 1930, on the centenary of the death of Bolívar, the government commissioned Mujica Millán for a full renovation of the pantheon. This time the pantheon was transformed in the Neocolonial style (fig. 2). It might seem paradoxical that the resting place for the hero that liberated a good portion of South America from the Spanish rule was renovated in an architectural style closely associated with colonial power; however, as architectural historian Silvia Hernández de Lasala explains, "The threat of a new colonialism, that of the United States, once the country had become the world's leading oil exporter, [Venezuela] looked back in an attempt to recover the image that only a few years earlier it had tried to suppress."[7] The successful completion of the pantheon established Mujica Millán's preeminence and led to a long career in Venezuela until he died in 1963. However, more importantly, it showcased the potential of employing visual repertoires from the Spanish colonial period to shape a new architectural style of power that embodied a modern national identity—a fast-growing country with a booming oil-based economy. The newly renovated pantheon made a clear statement indicating an anti-American, nationalist

Fig. 2. Manuel Mujica Millán, Panteón Nacional de Venezuela, 1930. Caracas, Venezuela. Postcard. Collection of the author. Photograph by and courtesy of the Denver Art Museum.

identity and set the first important architectural precedent for El Silencio.

Times of change

The year 1928 was one of dissent and protest in Venezuela. That February, a group of students from the Universidad Central de Venezuela la Semana del Estudiante (Student's Week) program participated in public demonstrations against the policies of the dictator Gómez. The regime brutally crushed the protest. More than two hundred members of the student movement, later known as "the generation of 1928," were imprisoned, sent to forced labor, or fled into exile. Nonetheless, the protest marked the beginning of change for a nation craving democracy and searching for a renewal of arts and culture; this moment brought the emergence of new figures in the arts and culture that shaped the post-Gómez era and the beginning of democracy in Venezuela.

Also, in 1928, Alfredo Boulton, a young heir of a prominent and very wealthy family, returned to Venezuela after five years of studying in Europe.[8] A photography and art enthusiast, Boulton became involved with the contemporary literary and artistic avant-garde, including the architect Carlos Raúl Villanueva (1900–1975), who moved to Caracas in 1929, and began to capture his own country in photographs. In the early 1930s, Boulton conceived the term belleza criolla, defined by the art critic Ariel Jiménez as "an idealized product of *mestizaje*, or racial mixing, among Blacks, whites, and Indigenous people, and thus an apt metaphor for American diversity and universal synthesis."[9] This vision was likely inspired by the influential 1925 book *La raza cósmica* published by the postrevolutionary Mexican intellectual José Vasconcelos.[10] He predicted the coming of a new age where happiness, love, imagination, and creativity would prevail thanks to the mixing of all the races, citing the examples of Mexico and Latin America. Vasconcelos's concept overlooked the destructive impact of European colonization on Indigenous peoples, but it still had an enormous influence across the region. His texts became central to many artists and intellectuals in Latin America, including Boulton who proposed with his belleza criolla a concept of national identity in the arts deeply intertwined with racial issues that were pressing to the public eye in the 1920s. His vision implicitly accepted and incorporated the European colonial past, in addition to Indigenous and African pasts, as essential for creating a modern Venezuela image, a new national image of power based on racial and cultural hybridity. Boulton's belleza criolla indicated a commitment to a larger nationalist project. This concept of cultural multiplicity also proved to be influential for Villanueva and his search for the roots of national identity in the architecture. Starting in the early 1930s, Boulton became Venezuela's most important patron for modern art. He supported and mentored artists aligned with his belleza criolla standards, such as the painter Armando Reverón (1889–1954) and the sculptor Francisco Narváez (1905–1982).

The future architect of El Silencio, Villanueva, was born in London to a Venezuelan diplomat and trained as an architect in Paris at the École de Beaux Arts. He visited his country for the first time in 1928.[11] The following year, Villanueva returned to settle in Venezuela and began his career as an architect at the Ministry of Public Works where he was appointed director of Buildings and Ornamental Constructions. As already mentioned, Villanueva soon befriended Boulton and other intellectuals and artists of his circle, such as the writer Arturo Uslar Pietri and Narváez. Although Villanueva is renowned for the strikingly modernist campus of the Universidad Central de Venezuela, one of Latin America's most successful midcentury modern architecture developments, his early works are firmly grounded in the French Beaux Arts tradition and the Neocolonial style.[12] For example, the overall design of his first park in Caracas, Carabobo Park from 1934, follows French formal park designs. However, the fountain and sculptures that embellish the grounds by Narváez, extolling the beauty of mixed-race peoples, are a celebration of Venezuelan identity aligned with Boulton's belleza criolla idea.

The Transition to Democracy

After the death of Gómez in December 1935, Eleazar López Contreras, an army general and close member of Gómez's entourage, was appointed president to transition the country to a democratic system. López Contreras surrounded himself with a group of young, well-educated, and experienced public servants who were gaining prominence in the final years of Gómez's regime. A central figure who emerged in the period and had a vast influence on the arts of post-Gomecism was the novelist mentioned above, journalist, politician, and lucid commentator in history: Arturo Uslar Pietri. He exerted an enormous impact on the different Venezuelan governments between 1939 and 1945, as minister of public instruction (1939–41), of finance (1943), and of the interior (1945), as well as secretary to the president from 1941 to 1943. Uslar Pietri was the first cousin, friend, and confidant of Boulton and a close friend of Villanueva. Uslar Pietri's first and best-known novel, *Las lanzas coloradas* (The Red Lances), was published in Madrid in 1931.[13] Now considered a classic of Latin American literature, the book abounds in nationalistic rhetoric. It narrates an epic account of a mestizo man who rebels against his white bosses during the independence war against Spain led by Bolívar, offering readers opportunities to consider the story in the light of the 1928 protest movement and the multiracial nature of Venezuelan society.

Fig. 3. Luis Malaussena and Carlos Raúl Villanueva, Venezuelan Pavilion for the Exposition Internationale des Arts et Techniques dans la Vie Moderne, 1937. Paris. Ville de Paris / Bibliothèque historique, 4C-EPF-006-02364. © The Regents of the University of California, The Bancroft Library, University of California, Berkeley. This work is made available under a Creative Commons Attribution 4.0 license.

Fig. 4. Luis Malaussena and Carlos Raúl Villanueva, *Columnas panzudas* for Venezuelan Pavilion for the Exposition Internationale des Arts et Techniques dans la Vie Moderne, 1937. Paris. Ville de Paris / Bibliothèque historique, 4C-EPF-006-02365.

In the first half of the twentieth century, there was a great deal of ambivalence about race in Venezuela. The official policy was one of racial equality with no legal discrimination or segregation. Indeed, according to the poet Andrés Eloy Blanco, the Venezuelan description of race was *café con leche* (coffee and milk): an expression referring to the racial composition of society.[14] The reality, however, was that Boulton, Villanueva, Uslar Pietri, and many of the intellectuals who shaped modern Venezuela belonged to an ambivalent elite which maintained a somatic image of themselves that emphasized their whiteness and European origins even while it validated Indigenous and Black cultural contributions by aligning with the idea of a deeply interracial society that resulted in a cultural fusion. This ambiguity, however, did not prevent them from reclaiming for themselves mixed-race origins in their search to formulate a new national identity paradigm aligned with Boulton's belleza criolla.

The new Venezuela that was emerging during the transition to democracy needed visual representations aligned with notions of change and modern nation building. Opting for the Neocolonial style, which had gained favor across Latin America since the late 1910s, became a suitable choice as the official architectural style for public buildings. The Exposition Internationale des Arts et Techniques dans la Vie Moderne (International Exhibition of Arts and Techniques in Modern Life), held from May to November of 1937 in Paris, offered the new Venezuelan government an unparalleled opportunity to showcase to the world the country's new face after decades of a brutal dictatorial regime. Following Mujica Millán's successful National Pantheon, the national pavilion was designed in the Neocolonial style by Luis Malaussena (1900–1963) and Villanueva, reinforcing the idea of a country grounded in history and tradition ready to face modern times.[15] It is important to mention that the 1915 Panama-California Exposition in San Diego, the 1922 Independence Centenary International Exposition in Rio de Janeiro, Brazil, the 1929 Exposición Iberoamericana (Iberoamerican

Exhibition) in Seville, Spain, as well as the 1935 California Pacific International Exposition in San Diego set important precedents in the use of neocolonial architecture for international fairs. In the case of Seville, some Latin American pavilions, especially the large and impressive neocolonial pavilions for Argentina by Martín Noel (1888–1963) and for Peru by Manuel Piqueras Cotolí (1885–1937)—who, like Mujica Millán, was born and trained in Spain—received extensive international praise and were widely published. In the case of the 1937 Venezuelan pavilion for Paris, the small building demonstrated many of the ideas and themes that Villanueva would further develop for El Silencio, notably the elaborate rococo portals (fig. 3) and the baluster-like *columnas panzudas*, or pot-bellied columns (fig. 4).

Fig. 5. Humphrey Nolan for Interamerica. Inc., Project rendering for the Tower of the Star at the Great National Fair, Caracas, 1939. Photograph of rendering by and courtesy of the Denver Art Museum.

Upon arriving in Venezuela in 1929, Villanueva undoubtedly observed a significant interest in colonial art and culture, particularly within cultured circles, including his new acquaintances, the Boulton family. The earliest collections of colonial art in Venezuela date from the second half of the 1800s when a small group of intellectuals and connoisseurs led by the writer and historian Arístides Rojas began gathering art and objects from the Spanish age.[16] The group slowly expanded in the early 1900s with a younger generation of collectors such as Luis Suárez Borges and John Boulton Rojas (Arístides Rojas's nephew and Alfredo Boulton's father), among others.[17] However, it was during the post-Gomecism period when interest in studying colonial art and culture expanded. The first museum exhibition of colonial art in Venezuela was organized in 1939 by the Ministry of Education at the Museum of Fine Arts in Caracas.[18] President López Contreras presided over the opening ceremony, and Uslar Pietri gave the opening remarks.[19] Three years later, in 1942, a group of colonial art collectors led by

Fig. 6. Gordon Bunshaft for Skidmore & Owings, Venezuelan Pavilion for the 1939 World's Fair. Photograph by Wurts Bros., New York, NY. X2010.7.1.7636. Museum of the City of New York.

the businessman Alfredo Machado Hernández founded the Asociación Venezolana Amigos del Arte Colonial and the Museo de Arte Colonial of Caracas to preserve and research the art of the Hispanic period.[20] The founding members were a mix of wealthy collectors and intellectuals, including Uslar Pietri and Villanueva; the latter played a central role in restoring a state-owned eighteenth-century mansion which President Isaías Medina Angarita designated to house the museum.[21] Contradictorily, the movement praising the European connection of the colonial past was led by some of the same intellectuals that extolled the multiracial nature of the country and its culture and praised Indigenous and Black cultures as central to it.

Fig. 7. Louis Skidmore holding the model of *Cacao* while sculptor Francisco Narváez works on the full-size sculpture for the Venezuelan Pavilion, 1939. Collection of the author. Photograph by and courtesy of the Denver Art Museum.

The writer Enrique Bernardo Núñez called Caracas "la ciudad de los techos rojos" (the city of red-tiled roofs) in 1947, and until that time—and despite Guzmán Blanco's urban interventions in the previous century—the city's architecture had changed very little from its colonial-era structures.[22] Under López Contreras's transition government, there was a strong drive to modernize all aspects of life and society, to catch up after years of paralysis. Invited by Venezuela's government in 1938, the French urban planner Maurice Rotival (1892–1980) submitted a project presenting a new encompassing vision for the capital.[23] In the so-called Plan Regulador (Regulatory Plan), Rotival, inspired by Haussmannian concepts, recommended the substitution of the bidirectional colonial square grid for a linear east-west grand central axis (Avenida Bolívar). He proposed a network of main roads along the valley and its surrounding peripheries, connecting to a monumental city center at its nucleus.[24] Villanueva was part of the team that worked with Rotival on the plan, a valuable experience for his proposal for El Silencio a few years later.

In the late 1930s, perhaps due to the Rotival plan and an influx of younger architects, architectural trends for official buildings transformed as modernist aesthetics were widely embraced, replacing the Neocolonial and other historical styles favored just a few years earlier. In addition to modernizing the urban imprint of the capital and showcasing affiliation with the latest international avant-garde trends in architecture, authorities were also looking for ways to present Venezuela as a modern country full of business opportunities. A new and distinct architectural language of power, devoid of historical references, emerged as war began in Europe. Among several projects that never materialized was the Great National Fair to be held in Caracas in 1939. American architect Humphrey Nolan (died 1977), working for Interamerica. Inc., proposed a modernist tower for the center of the exhibition grounds (fig. 5). However, it appears that, instead of the fair in Caracas, resources were channeled to present a large national pavilion at the 1939–40 New York World's Fair. The project was granted to the New York–based architecture firm Skidmore & Owings (from 1939, Skidmore, Owings & Merrill), which appointed Gordon Bunshaft (1909–1990) to develop the project.[25] Just three years after the Paris neocolonial pavilion, a modernist structure of glass and steel with a cantilevered roof offered a stark contrast (fig. 6). Art played a central aspect in the building. Artists Reverón and Narváez, both close to Boulton and Villanueva, received the art commissions for the pavilion (fig. 7).

El Silencio

In April 1941, Isaías Medina Angarita, a close ally of president López Contreras, was elected president of Venezuela. A charismatic leader, the president expanded the modernizing agenda of the previous government. He counted on a group of educated and experienced bureaucrats from the preceding administration, particularly Uslar Pietri, who was deeply involved in setting educational and cultural policies. With Europe at war, Medina Angarita launched an accelerated public works agenda infused with nationalistic overtones aimed to boost the country's economy, which was affected by the conflict. The modernization of the capital and the pressing need for affordable housing became central to the president's agenda. The urban renewal project for El Silencio neighborhood, initially included as part of the Regulatory Plan developed by Rotival, was originally planned as an area for government buildings. A different set of political priorities during the early 1940s might explain the Medina Angarita administration's decision to change the use of this valuable land at the heart of the city's business area to a residential area. The development of such a large housing complex at the city's center was unprecedented. In the 1930s and '40s, European and American urban planners advocated for housing areas on the peripheries of cities. This approach was embraced across Latin America, making El Silencio a notorious exception.

The agency in charge of the finances and oversight of the project was the Banco Obrero (Workers' Bank), a state bank founded in 1928 to finance public housing, which until the early 1940s was mostly limited to middle-income, single-family housing.[26] Due to the large scale of the development led by the Banco Obrero, funding exceeded the capacity of local banks. In seeking a loan from the Export-Import Bank of Washington, the president of the bank, Diego Nucete Sardi, successfully argued how politically and economically favorable the massive construction of housing was and also pointed out that it created much-needed employment opportunities during the middle of an economic downturn caused by World War II.[27] The Washington bank granted a loan of six million dollars with preferential conditions to start the project despite the difficulties of the ongoing war. It was a substantial loan for a country that generously supported the Allied forces with oil.

Due to the negative impact sustained from displacing all the inhabitants of an entire neighborhood, an unprecedented press campaign preceded the demolition work in hopes of defending the project. As Villanueva later commented on his work for the renovation of El Silencio, it was "a sanitation project in an unhealthy area in the heart of an old city."[28] National press showcased the area's misery, squalor, and poverty. Dramatic images of destitution and grime accompanied newspaper and magazine articles, highlighting the need for

Fig. 8. Alfredo Boulton, photograph of El Silencio, ca. 1945. Getty Research Institute. © J. Paul Getty Trust.

change in the area. The sector was home to 331 houses, of which forty-two were brothels; there were also forty-nine tenement houses, thirty-two liquor stores, nine lodging houses, and almost two hundred houses destined for other dubious purposes. Among the more than three thousand residents, there were 465 cases of tuberculosis and 2,327 cases of venereal disease.[29]

The Banco Obrero organized an architectural competition by invitation.[30] In March 1942, the two selected architects, Villanueva and Carlos Guinand, submitted their proposals. Villanueva's project recommended seven neocolonial-inspired buildings with apartments for middle-class families only. His plan included porticoes, pedestrian sidewalks, and gardens between the buildings. All the buildings were aligned with the street edge of each city block to keep the original grid structure of the colonial city. Guinand proposed a sleek modernist-style development, comprising eight buildings with apartments for working-class tenants and three for middle-class families, with commercial premises on the ground floors. Both projects followed Rotival's master plan for the area as requested by city authorities.

The government appointed a large commission of evaluators, including ministers, high-ranking government officials, developers, representatives of public utilities, and engineers, who recommended that Guinand and Villanueva should jointly develop a unified alternative with the positive aspects of both proposals. Both architects modified their projects, but each one was on his own, transforming them according to the commission's indications and presenting their projects again. On May 28, 1942, the commission ruled that Villanueva's design was the winner, but not before recognizing the "brilliant solutions" of Guinand's proposal, mentioning that "thanks to the solid qualities achieved by him since the first stage of the competition, his work served as a very useful basis for the result achieved."[31] Surprisingly, the commission selected a proposal whose historical architecture went against the grain of current government buildings, including the noted modernist Gran Colombia School (1939–42) in Caracas by Villanueva. The committee may have considered that incorporating elements from the traditional examples of Venezuelan architecture would garner greater acceptance among the future inhabitants of the complex because of their familiarity with the materials and styles. Moreover, the use of neocolonial architecture undoubtedly facilitated a more seamless integration into the existing historic urban context.

President Medina Angarita officially began the El Silencio demolition on July 25, 1942, the day the city was founded in 1567.[32] Without any doubt, El Silencio was an architectural and engineering tour de force. It was finished in thirty months despite requiring major infrastructure preparation, including channeling two creeks crossing the area. Due to seismic activity in Caracas, the structural aspects of the buildings needed special attention, and steel-reinforced concrete and modern manufactured materials and technologies were widely employed.

Despite the neocolonial exterior, Villanueva's proposal was modernist in spirit, with carefully studied circulation paths for people and automobiles. The final project was respectful of the surrounding colonial city and sought to smoothly integrate the massive volumes of the new buildings within the neighborhood's existing character, slowly changing the scale and proportion of the buildings as they move away from the main square (originally named Plaza General Rafael Urdaneta and, after 1952, Plaza Daniel Florencio O'Leary). Villanueva also provided ample public space with fountains as the proposal's core, another reference to colonial city planning (fig. 8).[33]

As previously mentioned, El Silencio's contradiction stands out: the use of the Neocolonial style for a government-funded development at the moment when president Medina Angarita was trying to distance himself from the Gómez and López Contreras administrations and aiming to project an image of a modern country that was building for the future. Perhaps Villanueva's discovery of colonial architecture upon his return to Venezuela was one of the main drivers for his choice, and he was able to persuade Uslar Pietri and others that this was the right choice for El Silencio due to its location at the center of the colonial city. It is not easy to trace the origin of Villanueva's deep interest in colonial architecture, mainly because he visited Venezuela for the first time as an adult. He had no early contact with colonial towns and never lived in a colonial house. However, it is evident that the experience of living for a few years in Venezuela profoundly changed his appreciation of the architecture of the Spanish age. In 1950, Villanueva published a book, *La Caracas de ayer y de hoy su arquitectura colonial y la reurbanización de "El Silencio"*—later expanded under the title *Caracas en tres tiempos* (Caracas in three moments) in 1966.[34] The lavishly illustrated book (with many photographs by Boulton) includes texts by himself, Carlos Manuel Möller, and Rotival. It offers a detailed study of colonial Caracas and sheds light on his appreciation of Venezuelan colonial architecture. In the preface to the second edition, Villanueva points out that "our ancestors knew how to be more sober, sincere and refined than us, in spite of the modest economic and social conditions in which they lived." He continues, "This work is a testimony of the permanence of the principles and norms that remained in colonial buildings; a collective Mea Culpa for having disregarded the legacy of our [Spanish] ancestors."[35]

Fig. 9. Alfredo Boulton, photograph of El Silencio, ca. 1945. Getty Research Institute. © J. Paul Getty Trust.

Fig. 10. Page from Alfredo Boulton's photographic album of El Silencio, showing sculptures by Francisco Narváez, ca. 1945. Getty Research Institute. © J. Paul Getty Trust.

The desire to recover the spirit of colonial Caracas is evident in the main square, Plaza O'Leary. In his book, Villanueva included several images of the old main square and market in Caracas, which was destroyed in 1864 by Guzmán Blanco while attempting to modernize the city.[36] In Villanueva's renovation, the porticoes, passageways, portals, and storefronts at the street level that surround Plaza O'Leary recall those of the old market in Caracas. They also create the right conditions for a lively street life, full of people and commercial activity, protected from the rain and the harsh tropical sun by the elegant porticoes, enabling a smooth transition between the road and the storefronts (fig. 9). On his comments on the project, the writer Mariano Picón Salas praised Villanueva's recovery of the knowledge of past Venezuelan architecture as an antidote to the "purely utilitarian beehive-buildings." He also mentioned that Villanueva's proposal for El Silencio bridges the modern with the glories of Spain and, by extension, with the ancient Mediterranean cultures.[37] The large and monumental square and surrounding buildings are also connected with Rotival's proposal for the area. The square marks the beginning of the east-west grand central axis known today as Avenida Bolívar.

Through study sketches, writings, and numerous photographs of notable examples of Venezuelan colonial architecture in his text, "The Meaning of Our Colonial Architecture," Villanueva showcased the importance of learning from the past while developing a new type of architecture adapted to the way of life and the geography of the country, mentioning that "at a time when the foundations of a contemporary Venezuelan architecture are being forged, it is opportune to look back to the past to unravel among the plastic elements of bygone days those that may still be valid today."[38] He also mentioned the importance of traditional construction materials and techniques, writing that "the functional sense of our colonial architecture must be recognized by the judicious use of the materials it employed."[39] For example, he referred to the *bahareque*, a seismic-resistant cane-and-mud constructive technique of the prehispanic era widely employed during the colonial period. The sense of place and the connections to local architectural history are also central considerations for Villanueva. For example, El Silencio's pot-belly columns are derived from eighteenth-century examples from a colonial mansion that once housed a girl's school. As Villanueva explained, "The past links with the future with the bulb-shaped motif of the columns at the Colegio Chávez."[40] He also paid homage to his family's colonial origins and history. The model for El Silencio's portals is based on the main entrance doorway of the ancestral Villanueva family house in the colonial town of San Carlos, in Venezuela.[41]

The monumental fountains by Narváez with allegorical figures of mestiza women, atop dolphins riding the waves, are also central to Villanueva's vision (fig. 10). Titled *Las Toninas* (pink river dolphins native to the Orinoco River), the fountains' subject is related to an Indigenous myth of fertility and prosperity, thus tying the myth to the foundational birth of a wealthy democratic nation. More than any other part of El Silencio, the sculptural groups embody the alignment of Villanueva's vision with Boulton's belleza criolla ideals. As Villanueva wrote in the book, "Modern urbanism inspires and stimulates the local genius: the young sculptor Narváez has been able to carve in stone the languor of the tropics."[42] Important public works, water fountains at the center of public squares were vital for daily colonial life and regarded as symbols of good government. As Villanueva explained, "The play of water in the fountains always expresses, as in the past, man's dominion over the elements of nature."[43] Beyond an ornamental purpose, the fountains represented an incredible display of water abundance and local culture at the center of the new community that surged from the debris of a dilapidated shanty town.

While the facades that faced the streets showcased the Neocolonial, the facades facing the internal courtyards and green areas were resolutely modernist (fig. 11). This apparent contradiction reveals Villanueva's interest and professional talent in postwar modernist architecture for social housing and his awareness of the importance of a careful integration with the surrounding colonial city. El Silencio predates more than a decade more ambitious large social housing developments such as the 23 de Enero complex with nine thousand apartments, completed from 1955 to 1958, where Villanueva fully expressed his modernist approach anchored in Swiss architect Le Corbusier's precepts for modern architecture.

Totaling 779 apartments and 201 commercial spaces, completed in record time in the middle of World War II, in a country with limited economic and technical resources, while simultaneously on the verge of a massive development period, El Silencio remains a historic milestone of Venezuelan architecture and Carlos Raúl Villanueva's genius. Villanueva pioneered a uniquely modern Venezuelan architecture by fusing colonial architectural vocabularies and ideas with international modernist concepts. This innovative approach emerged during Venezuela's rapid embrace of avant-garde modernism in the 1940s, creating a compelling bridge between the nation's rich historical heritage and its modern future. Still today, El Silencio embodies the nationalistic ideas and aspirations created by a small group of visionaries that shaped the origins of modern Venezuela.

Fig. 11. Alfredo Boulton, photograph of El Silencio, ca. 1945. Getty Research Institute. © J. Paul Getty Trust.

Notes

1. Ricardo de Sola Ricardo, *La reurbanización "El Silencio": crónica 1942-1945* (Caracas, Venezuela: E. Armitano Editor, 1988), 26. Unless otherwise noted, all translations by the author.

2. Leszek M. Zawisza, *Breve historia de los jardines en Venezuela* (Caracas, Venezuela: Oscar Todtmann Editores, 1990), 86.

3. On the late 1800s transformation of Latin American cities, see Idurre Alonso and Maristella Casciato, eds., *The Metropolis in Latin America 1830-1930: Cityscapes, Photographs, Debates* (Los Angeles: Getty Research Institute, 2021).

4. Hannia Gómez, *Suite Iberia* (Caracas, Venezuela: Sala TAC, Trasnocho Arte Contacto, 2015), 80–89.

5. Silvia Hernández de Lasala, *Venezuela entre dos siglos: la arquitectura de 1870 a 1930* (Caracas, Venezuela: Armitano Editores, 1997), 165.

6. Ibid., 166.

7. Ibid.

8. On Boulton, see Juan Manuel Bonet, et al., *Boulton Moderno: 1928-1944* (Barcelona: RM Verlag, 2014) and "Boulton, Alfredo," in *Diccionario biográfico de las artes visuales en Venezuela*, ed. Francisco Da Antonio, et al. (Caracas, Venezuela: Fundación Galería de Arte Nacional, Fundación Cisneros, Fundación Para la Cultura Urbana, 2005), 1:202–4.

9. Ariel Jiménez, "Figuring Venezuela, 1912–1949," in *Alfredo Boulton and His Contemporaries: Critical Dialogues in Venezuelan Art, 1912–1974*, edited by Ariel Jiménez (New York: The Museum of Modern Art, 2008), 85.

10. José Vasconcelos, *La raza cósmica: misión de la raza iberoamericana: notas de viajes a la América de Sur* (Paris: Agencia mundial de librería, 1925).

11. "Villanueva, Carlos Raúl," in *Diccionario de historia de Venezuela* (Caracas, Venezuela: Fundación Empresas Polar, 2010), 4:269–70.

12. On Villanueva's University Campus, see Silvia Hernández de Lasala, *En busca de lo sublime: Villanueva y la Ciudad Universitaria de Caracas* (Caracas: Universidad Central de Venezuela, 2006).

13. Arturo Uslar Pietri, *Las lanzas coloradas* (Madrid: Zeus Editorial, 1931).

14. See Winthrop R. Wright, *Café con leche: Race, Class, and National Image in Venezuela* (Austin: University of Texas Press, 1990).

15. Valerie Fraser, *Building the New World: Studies in the Modern Architecture of Latin America, 1930–1960* (London: Verso, 2000), 96–97.

16. Carlos F. Duarte, *El museo de arte colonial de Caracas, Quinta de Anauco* (Caracas, Venezuela: Ernesto Armitano, Editor, 1991), 11.

17. Ibid.

18. Ibid., 14.

19. Ibid., 13.

20. Ibid., 14.

21. Ibid.

22. Enrique Bernardo Núñez, *La ciudad de los techos rojos: calles y esquinas de Caracas* (Caracas, Venezuela: Tiporafía de Vargas, 1947).

23. Maurice E. H. Rotival, "Caracas marcha hacia Adelante," in *Caracas en tres tiempos: iconografía retrospectiva de una ciudad*, ed. Carlos Raúl Villanueva, et al. (Caracas, Venezuela: Ediciones Comisión Asuntos Culturales del Cuatricentenario de Caracas, 1966), 171–82.

24. On Rotival's plan for Caracas, see Marta Vallmitjana, *El Plan Rotival: la Caracas que no fue: 1939-1989 un plan urbano para Caracas* (Caracas: Caracas Ediciones Instituto de Urbanismo, Facultad de Arquitectura y Urbanismo, Universidad Central de Venezuela, 1991).

25. Frank Monaghan, *Official Guide Book of the New York World's Fair* (New York: Exposition Publications, 1939), 117.

26. "Bancos," in *Diccionario de historia*, 1:351.

27. Juan José Pérez Rancel, "70 años de la inauguración de la Reurbanización El Silencio," *Entrerayas: la revista de Arquitectura*, August 26, 2015, https://entrerayas.com/2015/08/70-anos-de-la-inauguracion-de-la-reurbanizacion-el-silencio/#more-23338.

28. Carlos Raúl Villanueva, "Reurbanización de El Silencio," in *Caracas en tres tiempos*, 183.

29. De Sola Ricardo, *La reurbanización "El Silencio,"* 53.

30. Ibid., 76–93.

31. Ibid., 78.

32. Ibid., 66–69.

33. Villanueva, "Reurbanización de El Silencio," 189.

34. Carlos Raúl Villanueva, et al., *La Caracas de ayer y de hoy: su arquitectura colonial y la reurbanización de "El Silencio"* (Paris: Draeger Frères, 1950) and Villanueva, et al., *Caracas en tres tiempos*.

35. Villanueva, "Introducción" in Villanueva, et al., *Caracas en tres tiempos*, 9.

36. Ibid., 74–76.

37. Mariano Picón Salas, "Caracas allí está," in Villanueva, et al., *Caracas en tres tiempos*, 13.

38. Carlos Raúl Villanueva, "El Sentido de nuestra arquitectura colonial," in Villanueva, et al., *Caracas en tres tiempos*, 37.

39. Ibid.

40. Villanueva, "Reurbanización de El Silencio," 190.

41. Ibid., 183.

42. Ibid., 200.

43. Ibid., 198.

LYNDA KLICH

Casa Zuno: Revolutionary *Gesamtkunstwerk*

To traverse the portal of Casa Zuno, amidst the leafy blocks of what is today the Colonia Americana in Guadalajara, is to find oneself outside of place and time. Its ornate facade, faced with tezontle—a porous, oxidized, volcanic rock in varying shades of red—and embellished with a lighter carved stone, is unlike any of the other luxurious private homes in the neighborhood and was so even at the time of its conception and construction, from 1922 to 1926 (fig. 1). The grounds, and then the building, completely envelop the visitor in rich, decorative forms. From the large carved wooden doors to the ornate furniture, from the walls, each painted in a different pastel palette, to the arched interior corridors, from the multilevel roof terraces to the garden with tiled fountains and benches, every element works to turn this private home into an immersive space. The allover design, however, is not merely experiential. It also signals a deliberate cultural, political, and social formation, through the Neocolonial style, that embeds dominant classed and raced hierarchies as key to molding an idealized, modern, revolutionary, Mexican citizen.

In bringing the concept of the *Gesamtkunstwerk*—the allover work of art—to Casa Zuno, I mean the term to take on a multivalence that speaks to how this home may have resonated within the context of postrevolutionary Mexico. On the level of aesthetics, of course, the synthesis of interior, exterior, and design elements handily meets the definition of a Gesamtkunstwerk. More importantly, however, on another level, the home encapsulates concepts of *mexicanidad*, or cultural expressions of a national identity, that had currency in the earliest years following the civil war of 1910–20. Each aspect of the building comes together in a type of national design program, a home ideally aestheticized according to prevailing postrevolutionary dictates that sought to negotiate Mexico's mestizo identity, which at that time was conceptualized as a mixture of Indigenous Mexican and Spanish heritages that erased completely African and Asian heritages.[1] Finally, Casa Zuno signifies as a Gesamtkunstwerk because it embodies the tensions that emerged from ideological attempts to model national citizenry by reconciling Mexico's Indigenous popular classes—signified by artisan labor—and the intellectual elite-*criollo* classes—signified by the neocolonial framework.

José Guadalupe Zuno Hernández commissioned this private residence in the state capital just as he began serving as governor of

Fig. 1. Postcard depicting Casa Zuno, ca. 1926. Photograph on card stock, 3½ × 5½ in. (8.9 × 12.7 cm). Collection of the author.

Jalisco in early 1923.[2] Led by the Guadalajaran engineer Arnulfo Villaseñor, the construction and decoration of Casa Zuno was a collaboration among fine artists by then prominent or gaining notice in Mexico City, including Dr. Atl (1875–1964) and Amado de la Cueva (1891–1926) both natives of Guadalajara, and David Alfaro Siqueiros and Xavier Guerrero (both 1896–1974), among others, as well as fine artists then active in Guadalajara, notably Carlos Orozco Romero (1898–1984), and finally, local artisans, most of whom remain unrecorded and, therefore, unacknowledged. The idea of Gesamtkunstwerk as home fits the personality, career, and aims of its patron, Zuno. A fascinating polymath, Zuno was also a naturalist, journalist, caricaturist, painter, editor, teacher, and lawyer, in addition to being a leading politician.

Casa Zuno sits on a large quarter-block corner lot in what was then called the Colonia Reforma, in the midst of a spacious garden, surrounded by a fence with stone columns that connect undulating walls, also faced with tezontle. The home's two-story tower stands prominently in the southwest corner of the lot, facing the intersection of Avenidas Uníon and del Bosque, the latter street today named for Zuno (fig. 2). This tallest part of the house contains two levels of pilastered and iron-grilled windows, as well as two carved cartouches (one identifying the dates of construction and another speaking to the moment of the Conquest). The tower is topped by a corner niche containing a cherub statue in a Greco-Roman style.[3]

Two declining facades extend from the tower, framing the domestic spaces. The principal facade (on Avenida del Bosque) is further embellished by a portico with Salomonic columns and enormous carved doors. Inside Casa Zuno's main gate, the house has two additional prominent facades. One faces east, toward the freestanding garage and office, and the other faces north, onto the garden, which is spotted with several tiled fountains (fig. 3). Both facades are covered with tezontle, pilastered and gated windows, and varied degrees of decoration, and each contains a prominent staircase. The interior rooms are set around an arcaded central courtyard, with entrances from the south—through a *zaguán*, or vestibule—and from the east, through a *recibidor*, or drawing room. The prominent library and living room run along the front of the house, with Zuno's private bedroom tucked into the corner; the family bedrooms, all connected, run along the west. Zuno's main receiving salon dominates the northern wing; at east is the large kitchen and guestroom. An elaborate staircase on the eastern side of the central patio leads to several *azoteas*, or rooftop patios, at various levels, providing views and respite (fig. 4). One, adorned with symbols of the hunt (a favorite pastime of Zuno), leads to what were then Zuno's studio and a meeting room.

As a patron, Zuno wanted his home to signal modernity, in line with his progressive policies for Jalisco.[4] In choosing the colonial revival style, or the Neocolonial, for his home, Zuno made a particularly deliberate statement, differentiating his home from the then-predominate local style for domestic architecture: a French-inflected style known as chalet. Pressed by his artist-collaborators, Zuno settled on the Neocolonial style, although he was wary of the costs such an elaborate structure entailed, because he considered it important to build in a "nationalist" style in differentiation to the "super ugly Italianate and Yankified" homes that "infested" Guadalajara, to use Zuno's own words.[5] The home's architectural language instead evokes, without exactly imitating, eighteenth-century palatial residences in Mexico City, such as the houses of the Mayorazgo de Guerrero on Calle Moneda.

Despite Zuno's attention to state issues, his home makes clear his allegiance to a larger, nationalist project. Neocolonial aesthetics were championed by several of his artist-collaborators, then working toward implementing the programs of José Vasconcelos, minister of education for President Álvaro Obregón and architect of the postrevolutionary cultural nation-building

Left: Fig. 2. Casa Zuno, view from the southwest, 1920s. Reproduced from *La casa de tezontle: monografía de la casa Zuno* (Guadalajara, Mexico: Universidad de Guadalajara, 1998), 6.

Below: Fig. 3. Casa Zuno, north facade and garden, 1930s. Reproduced from *La casa de tezontle: monografía de la casa Zuno* (Guadalajara, Mexico: Universidad de Guadalajara, 1998), 21.

project. One of the first such official structures, the Mexican pavilion at the 1922 Exposição Internacional do Centenario da Independencia (International Exhibition of the Centenary of Independence) in Rio de Janeiro, sanctioned the formulation of modern Mexican identity though the neocolonial architectural language that would find an echo in Casa Zuno, with grand, retablo-like portals, mixed-line crowns, iron-grilled windows with ornamental frames, pilastered corners, upper-story niches with sculptures, and profuse surface carving (fig. 5).[6] On the international stage, the Neocolonial signaled back to a supposedly more stable and refined Mexico, countering its reputation as a brutal and barbaric state that the revolution had earned it. On the national front, Vasconcelos repurposed colonial buildings or constructed neocolonial buildings, including his ministry's headquarters, several primary schools, and a national stadium, all in the works around the same time as Casa Zuno.[7]

Many other scholars have demonstrated that the recuperation of the Neocolonial, however, had begun earlier, as far back as Manuel G. Revilla's 1893 study of ancient and colonial art, as an antidote to the austere Neoclassicism deployed during the decades-long regime of Porfirio Díaz.[8] The promotion of the Neocolonial style continued during the revolution and beyond, notably in the writings, teachings, and lectures of the architect Federico

Fig. 4. Casa Zuno, central patio, completed 1926. Photograph by the author (2022).

Fig. 5. Postcard depicting Mexican Pavilion for *Exposicão do Centenario* (International Exhibition of the Centenary of Independence), Rio de Janeiro, 1922. Carlos Obregón Santacilia and Carlos Tarditi, architects. Photolithograph on card stock, 3½ × 5½ in. (8.9 × 12.7 cm). Collection of the author.

Mariscal (1881–1971), longtime colleague of Vasconcelos's who shared ideas in the Ateneo de la Juventud, an organization of young cultural leaders. For proponents of the Neocolonial, the style embodied *mestizaje*, the racial and cultural mixing that characterized Mexico, framing national identity only around the Spanish (represented by the architectural forms) and the Indigenous (manifested in the labor and the ornamental elements). In reviving the colonial style for the modern, postrevolutionary state, proponents found in the Neocolonial the perfect paradigm of a national "hybridization."

Of course, despite the acknowledgment of the Indigenous contributions to Mexican culture and identity, the Neocolonial remains an architecture of power, a dynamic clearly laid out in the writing of Vasconcelos, the most visible proponent of mestizaje as national identity. Vasconcelos had developed these ideas in writings and lectures during the teens, and they came together most notably in his 1925 publication *La raza cósmica*. For Vasconcelos, the Conquest did not signal the imposition of hegemony; rather, it provided the "spiritual and cultural foundations of Hispanoamérica."[9] Mestizaje served as the mechanism for using Western cultural, moral, and civilizing forces to uplift what was commonly understood as the "pure and instinctual" Indigenous peoples, making their incorporation into the modern nation—both symbolically and actually—palatable for ruling elites faced with the populist social processes of the revolution.[10] In *La raza cósmica*, Vasconcelos frames mestizaje in a way that precisely fitted the Neocolonial: the Indigenous contribution could only be activated by the transformational engine of the Spanish. "Even the pure Indians are Hispanized," he writes, "The Indian has no other door to the future but the door of modern culture, nor any other road but the road already cleared by Latin civilization."[11] In advancing ideas about the

Fig. 6. Casa Zuno, west facade, detail of upper cartouche, completed 1926. Photograph by the author (2022).

Left: Fig. 7. *Untitled (Facade columns, Santa Mónica, Guadalajara)*, 1926. Photograph by Edward Weston. © Center for Creative Photography, Arizona Board of Regents.

Right: Fig. 8. Casa Zuno, south facade, detail of porch columns, completed 1926. Photograph by the author (2022).

Fig. 9. Xoloitzcuintle detail on courtyard arch at Zuno's house, 1926. Photograph by Edward Weston. Jean Charlot Collection and Archives, University of Hawai'i at Manoa. © Center for Creative Photography, Arizona Board of Regents.

Fig. 10. Interior doorframes at Zuno's house, 1926. Photograph by Edward Weston. Jean Charlot Collection and Archives, University of Hawai'i at Manoa. © Center for Creative Photography, Arizona Board of Regents.

Fig. 11. *Unititled (Ceiling mural at Zuno's House)*, 1926. Photograph by Edward Weston. © Center for Creative Photography, Arizona Board of Regents.

Neocolonial as national metaphor, Vasconcelos and others continued a long history of what Ángel Rama has termed the *letrado*, those who occupied privileged social, political, and cultural positions thanks to their educated status (**typically white or white-identifying elites**).[12] Bringing that term into the postrevolutionary period, Carlos Monsiváis has classified thinkers like Vasconcelos and Zuno **as a "merit aristocracy," which believes that a superiority of character has destined it to lead.**[13]

In ideologically coded speeches and writings around the official neocolonial buildings popping up around Mexico City, Vasconcelos and other intellectuals made clear their redemptory potential: the arcades and interior spaces accorded with modern concepts of education, and the linking of indoor and outdoor areas in particular provided a model for healthy living, a line of thought perhaps echoed in the extensive gardens at Casa Zuno.[14] In line with national neocolonial rhetoric, outdoor spaces connected with the uplifting and transformation of Indigenous populations.[15] **Whatever their purposes, these buildings contributed to a disciplinary spatial politics that viewed Indigenous peoples as needing to be rescued from their unsanitary lives, customs, and practices.**

The upper cartouche on the western facade of Casa Zuno declares the patron's adherence to these then widely current ideas (fig. 6). It depicts the precise moment of the Conquest at the foundation of Vasconcelos's concept of mestizaje, embodied in the peaceful meeting of a Spanish conquistador and an Indigenous ruler, who stand on top of a jaguar, a representation of Mesoamerican aggression and power, here vanquished.[16] Mestizaje is then embedded throughout the architecture and decoration of Casa Zuno. Like in the theories of Vasconcelos and others, Spanish elements obviously dominate, and several elements even emulate existing colonial structures. For example, the lavish facade columns, abundant with twisting vines, bunches of grapes, and leaves, pay homage to Santa Mónica, a prominent local Augustinian convent church from the early eighteenth century (figs. 7 and 8). Casa Zuno is somewhat of a temporal and stylistic pastiche, which Cristina López Uribe has wittily called "an unusual experiment in the application of Neocolonial principles."[17] Nonetheless, the overriding colonial reference is the sumptuous architecture of the eighteenth-century palaces built by Spanish nobles in the historic center of Mexico City and fueled by wealth generated by mining, agricultural, and mercantile pursuits (and, of course, Indigenous labor).[18] These *palacios señoriales* (stately palaces) were quite obviously designed to declare their wealth, as the early-twentieth-century colonial art historian Manuel Toussaint noted long ago.[19]

Several elements insert the Indigenous presence into Casa Zuno, including the tiled and gated staircase in the central patio (see fig. 4). Its undulating rail purportedly references the body of Quetzalcoatl, the Mesoamerican god embodied as the feathered serpent. (Among his many other contributions, Quetzalcoatl fostered the cultivation of the food staple maize and developed the art of stone carving; there is a carved ear of corn at top of the staircase.)[20] Referencing the ancient belief that Quetzalcoatl's spirit twin, Xolotl, who had the face of a dog, led the god and the sun every night to Mictlán, where the sun died, the back of the staircase contains relief carvings of a Xoloitzcuintle, guard to the living and guide to the dead (fig. 9). Quetzalcoatl, who led the sun out of Mictlán every dawn, also governed the science of astronomy, and Casa Zuno's construction emulates the Mesoamerican architectural practice of aligning structures with astronomical events. The staircase is oriented precisely so that during the vernal equinox in March, the sun seemingly falls down the rail. These references, if opaque, abstract indigeneity within the mestizo and line up with Vasconcelean framing of ancient Mexico as the pure and natural soul of modern Mexico.

The location of the Indigenous aspect of mestizaje in folk art by postrevolutionary intellectuals also falls in line with these ideas. Casa Zuno specifically participates in this dialogue through the walls of its rooms, each painted in

Fig. 12. Decorations in Sala de Discusiones Libres (former monastery of San Pedro y San Pablo; today Museo de las Constituciones) with Roberto Montenegro mural, *El árbol de la vida*, in background, 1922. Jean Charlot Collection and Archives, University of Hawai'i at Manoa.

Fig. 13. Casa Zuno, interior courtyard, overdoor panels with Tonalá tiles, completed 1926. Photograph by the author (2022).

a different pastel color (pink, green, blue), with profusely ornamented fresco designs containing flora, fauna, and cosmological elements (sun, moon, stars). They frame the doorways and windows, trim the ceilings, and surround the overhead lights, thought to have been painted by Guerrero, Siqueiros, de la Cueva, and others (figs. 10 and 11).[21] Dismissed by some scholars as mere decoration, these paintings meaningfully contribute to the overall integration of form and meaning in Casa Zuno, ideologically aligning with mestizaje as visualized in contemporary Mexican art.

Specifically, Casa Zuno's interior decorations stage a style that I call decorative nationalism.[22] Exemplified by the intricate sinuosity found at Casa Zuno, decorative nationalism—which was then practiced by Vasconcelos's favored artists, including Roberto Montenegro (1887–1968) and Adolfo Best Maugard (1891–1965)—accomplished two things as judged by its proponents: it married Mesoamerican and Spanish colonial forms in an updated, modern visual language, and it represented Mexico as a refined and beautiful place. In the process, of course, as scholars such as Karen Cordero Reiman and Olivier Debroise have long noted, decorative nationalism posits Mexico in an otherworldly, mythic, and allegorical light, distant from revolutionary carnage and societal inequities.[23] Decorative nationalism transformed San Pedro y San Pablo, a deconsecrated Jesuit church refashioned as an assembly hall for the working classes (that is, Indigenous and mestizo Mexicans) by Vasconcelos in one of his first commissions. Inside, the Sala de Discusiones Libres contains profuse decorative trimming of garlands filled with pomegranates, birds, and floral varieties, created by a team of artists that included Guerrero (fig. 12).[24] As the first postrevolutionary pictorial language, decorative nationalism complemented neocolonial architecture seamlessly. As architectural decoration, it enveloped those who entered in a soothing and beautiful space, aiming to uplift and edify the Indigenous working classes.[25]

Jalisco *artesanía* played a central role in the folk arts revival that drove decorative nationalism, beginning with events to mark the centennial of independence in 1921, such as the expansive *Exposición de Artes Populares*. Particularly visible were the state's distinctive tile and ceramics, especially those from Tonalá, a town about ten miles southeast of Casa Zuno, that form the overdoor panel decorations on the front porch and the interior courtyard doors, as well as interior and exterior wainscotting (fig. 13). The *Artes Populares* catalog authors declared Tonalan ceramics—characterized by whimsical designs featuring animals and vegetation in strong linearity and varied colors on a terra cotta background—to have the most important "artistic value" in Mexico, partially due to Tonalá's status as a thriving pre-Conquest ceramics center (fig. 14). Typifying the patriarchal framing of such national endeavors, *Artes Populares* considered Tonalá ceramics proof of the exemplary character of the town's "peaceful and gentle" citizens who industriously and collectively contributed to the town's economy by creating this work.[26]

Tonalan ceramics also provided a source for Best Maugard's painting style, which became codified as a national mode through a drawing method taught at public schools (and was instituted by Zuno in Jalisco in 1923).[27] It also appeared in the elaborate stage settings for large-scale public events, such as the Noche Mexicana, a spectacle of folk art and dance held in Chapultepec Park in September 1921, and for the independence centennial that same year. One of the ten pavilions mounted for the event that showcased artisanal work was solely dedicated to ceramics from Jalisco.[28] For proponents of decorative nationalism, folk art, with its "hybrid decorative combinations" of Spanish and ancient craftsmanship, was evidence of mestizaje and was a respectable way to showcase Mexico's national character, improving upon pottery exhumed from archaeological sites.[29] In the words of the poet José Juan Tablada, a staunch promoter of the style during his years as a cultural attaché in New York, decorative nationalism proved that the nation's soul was "buried in the brown skin of the people."[30]

Casa Zuno's monumental, carved wood doors stand as one of the building's most public-facing declarations of a national authenticity rooted in mestizaje (fig. 15). From the earliest years of the postrevolutionary period, vanguard artists advanced the woodcut, a physical printmaking medium that can include sharply angled, roughhewn forms, as a revolutionary art form. Artists deployed the medium as a sign of class solidarity, an association spurred by the aesthetic suggestion of a primitivized,

Fig. 14. *Olla*, from Tonalá, Jalisco, ca. 1920. Polished and polychromed ceramic. Museo Nacional de Arte, Mexico City: Colección de Arte Popular "Roberto Montenegro."

Fig. 15. Casa Zuno, front doors, ca. 1926. Carved by Juan Hernández. Photograph by the author (2022).

Fig. 16. Gabriel Fernández Ledesma, *Escultura y talla directa*, 1928. Woodcut, 12⅜ × 12½ in. (31.2 × 31.7 cm). Colección Andrés Blaisten/Fondo Francisco Díaz de León.

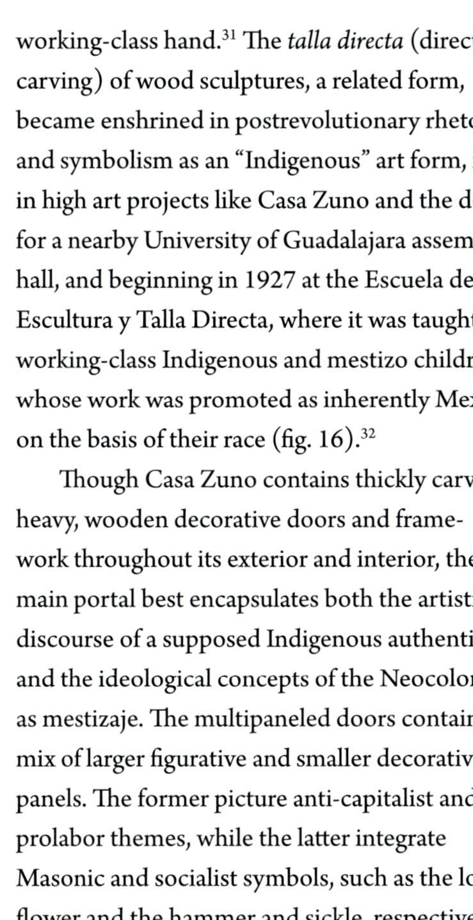

working-class hand.[31] The *talla directa* (direct carving) of wood sculptures, a related form, became enshrined in postrevolutionary rhetoric and symbolism as an "Indigenous" art form, first in high art projects like Casa Zuno and the doors for a nearby University of Guadalajara assembly hall, and beginning in 1927 at the Escuela de Escultura y Talla Directa, where it was taught to working-class Indigenous and mestizo children whose work was promoted as inherently Mexican on the basis of their race (fig. 16).[32]

Though Casa Zuno contains thickly carved, heavy, wooden decorative doors and framework throughout its exterior and interior, the main portal best encapsulates both the artistic discourse of a supposed Indigenous authenticity and the ideological concepts of the Neocolonial as mestizaje. The multipaneled doors contain a mix of larger figurative and smaller decorative panels. The former picture anti-capitalist and prolabor themes, while the latter integrate Masonic and socialist symbols, such as the lotus flower and the hammer and sickle, respectively.[33] Arranged around visual and iconographical symmetry, the door contains two central square panels with figures seated in a lotus position—an Indigenous female corn/fertility goddess at left and an Indigenous male reading a book and holding a hammer and sickle at right—surrounded by natural and cosmological elements. Long horizontal panels above and below render contrasts in gender-based values that can perhaps be read as behavioral lessons and/or moral choices. At top recline competing archetypes of femininity: decadence embodied by a wealthy woman, her sexual availability signaled by the breasts that peek out from her dress, and maternity, an upstanding figure who envelopes and nurtures her offspring, the naturalness of her brand of femininity encoded by the vegetation surrounding her. At bottom, their masculine counterpoints: at left, a humble, similarly naturalized campesino pauses from working the land to quench his thirst (fig. 17); next to him, the sated, wealthy landowner greedily accumulates wealth, an empty bottle, presumably from alcohol, laying by his side, signals his moral decline. Eight smaller rectangular panels below contain varied scenes of postrevolutionary reform, such as rural education, socialist emblems and slogans, battling soldiers, and figures suggesting naturalized indigeneity, all peppered with Masonic symbolism. A small but significant detail, a doorknocker emblazoned with a hammer and sickle, announces Zuno's public commitment to the working classes and the progressive turn initiated by his administration.[34]

Overall, like the pictorial strategies of the sixteenth-century mendicant friars used to catechize the nonlettered and to overcome language barriers with Indigenous peoples, the doors speak to the edification of the model revolutionary citizen. The revolutionary evangelism through pictorial wood carvings also exemplifies the wood bench in Casa Zuno's library (fig. 18). Part of an overall decorative schema of the library, the space in the home most overtly dedicated to nurturing the mind (fig. 19), the bench has four panels that feature scenes of idealized, if unrealized, postrevolutionary reform and Indigenous pride. From left to right: a lively classroom scene shows students being educated about the class struggle, the strategically placed text banner evoking at once the voice scroll from Mesoamerican codices and the ribbon banners from colonial painting (fig. 20); next, in a call to action, a group of protesting urban workers brandish tools-cum-weapons-cum-socialist symbols, followed by triumphant revolutionary soldiers, and finally, campesinos productively working what is presumably reappropriated land. Integrated among the rocaille, decorative elements such as corn, sun, moon, and, again,

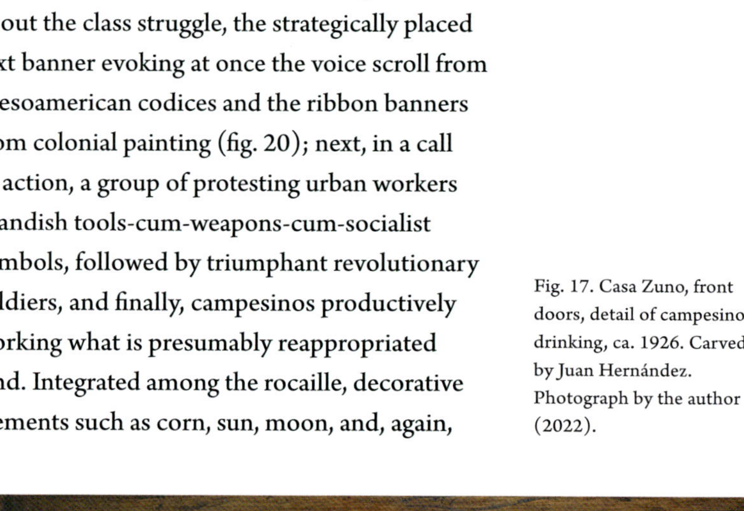

Fig. 17. Casa Zuno, front doors, detail of campesino drinking, ca. 1926. Carved by Juan Hernández. Photograph by the author (2022).

Fig. 18. Casa Zuno, bench from library, ca. 1926. Carved by Juan Hernández. Photograph by the author (2022).

the feathered serpent (which runs down the sides of the back, along the arms, to the legs, where it culminates in a foot design) nod to Indigenous Mexico.

The idea of edifying through image and the strategy of pitting the moral characters of the working class and elite against each other relate directly to strategies then employed by muralists. While these scenes are in dialogue with the murals in the most important official buildings in the capital, Mexico City, their decorative framing evokes not the sobriety of monastic architecture, or a messianic mission, but rather the baroque exuberance that characterized the domestic and church furniture that broadcasted wealth in the noble houses and marked ecclesiastical authority. Like the murals in neocolonial buildings, these scenes and elements fit within an overarching framework that speaks of authority and power, encoding and maintaining the hierarchical balance ultimately desired by the intelligentsia, monied, and empowered classes, reminders that the education and social actions of the Indigenous and mestizo working classes took place within the patriarchal frameworks of the postrevolutionary elite.

Fig. 19. Casa Zuno, view of library, ca. 1920s. Reproduced from *La casa de tezontle: monografía de la casa Zuno* (Guadalajara, Mexico: Universidad de Guadalajara, 1998), 59.

The dynamics of Casa Zuno's construction encapsulate the classed tensions of postrevolutionary rhetoric and cultural practices, where the "merit autocracy" articulated revolutionary ideals that seldom became lived reality, and the valorizing of Indigenous peoples, traditions, and cultures largely remained symbolic. Of the many local Indigenous builders and artisans who worked on the house, the names of only two remain known (one only partially). Juan Hernández, a local craftsman, carved the doors, the bench, and a gunrack for Zuno's study, following designs by Guerrero, de la Cueva, and Zuno himself. A stone carver, recalled by Zuno only with his given name, Alberto, modeled the porch columns after those at Santa Mónica.[35] The framing of their artisan abilities—as the labor provided to enact the ideas articulated by the intellectual elite—speaks to the hierarchies inherent in postrevolutionary nation building, modeling the rhetoric of Vasconcelean mestizaje, in which Western culture and intellect elevates Indigenous instinct and natural talent. The artist Gabriel Fernández Ledesma (1904–1984), for example, discussed Hernández as remarkably "theory free" driven only by an "organic necessity" to express himself in a pure way.[36] In his patriarchal recollections of Alberto's work, Zuno remembered that his team found the carver begging in the street and recruited him to work on the columns, praising Alberto's ability to take a drawing and "translate it with . . . exactitude."[37] In relegating Indigenous artisans to places of labor and manual technique, these patrons, thinkers, and artists—no matter how progressive their politics—paradoxically replicated the power relationships that created the colonial monuments they modeled, as a statement by Dr. Atl makes clear: "The constant influence of the skill and feeling of the indigenous workers who built the churches, palaces, houses and votive monuments . . . form the genuine representation of colonial art."[38] These dynamics and the rhetoric around Indigenous artistic labor diminish it and ignore the centuries of received knowledge that it embodies and that made possible neocolonial structures and their original models.

Fig. 20. Panel from bench from Casa Zuno library showing classroom, ca. 1926. Carved by Juan Hernández. Photograph by the author (2022).

Casa Zuno exists only because of Zuno's wealth and power, perhaps an obvious statement, but one that should not be minimized, especially in a dialogue about the Neocolonial. Indeed, Zuno recalled how, despite widespread shortages that deterred his postrevolutionary civil reconstruction projects, which sought to better the daily life of all Jalisco's inhabitants, suppliers readily agreed to provide materials for the governor's private home expeditiously—and at cost—including brick and stone for the structure and decoration, tezontle from the nearby Tequila volcano for facing, cedar and other woods for the doors, furniture, molding, wainscotting, and floors, iron for the grilles, and tiles for the overdoor panels and wainscoting. Nonetheless, Zuno bristled when accused by his detractors of creating a space that expressed "his adoption of bourgeois ways" and showed the "spirit of the nouveau riche."[39]

In their 1923 manifesto, the Technical Workers, Painters, and Sculptors Union, peopled by Mexico's foremost artists (including several who worked on Casa Zuno), famously declared allegiance with workers and vowed to overturn the "old, cruel order" that subjugated them. The admirable collectivity of Casa Zuno, in which artists' authorship attaches to elements of the home only by carried-down anecdote, embodies a type of monumental art well-fitted to what the artists called their "aesthetic-educational struggle."[40] The deliberate design of Casa Zuno's architecture, spaces, fittings, and decoration translates revolutionary zeal into visual form, or what the artists called "the healthiest spiritual expression" of Mexico. As a postrevolutionary Gesamtkunstwerk, Casa Zuno, in essence, is a place of national storytelling and social formation. As a private individual's home filled with politicized discourse, however, it contains what Renato González Mello has called an "ambiguity between the public and the private."[41] Every element of Casa Zuno unites to take it beyond being the home of one nuclear family to instead becoming a showpiece for the regeneration of the new revolutionary nation. As such, Casa Zuno models the paradoxes of its time, in which artists sought to define mexicanidad through the symbolic incorporation of Mexico's Indigenous cultural heritage into a modern, national identity. In so doing, Casa Zuno encapsulates the problematics of the Neocolonial as a model for that identity, demonstrating how, despite a noble belief in the ideas—by visualizing the tensions between decorative and political, the criollo and the Indigenous, the elite and the laboring sectors of society—the Neocolonial style embedded classed and raced hierarchies into the built environment and daily life.

Notes

1. I thank Christina de León for a conversation that helped me formulate this terminology. This essay also benefitted from comments from Anna Indych-López and Tara Zanardi, and from my colleagues and the audience at the Denver Art Museum symposium that originated this publication. I also thank Guillermo Ortega Vázquez and Alicia Villarreal for their assistance and our conversations during my visit to Casa Zuno in August 2022, and Joseph Shaikewitz for research support.

2. Zuno recalls the circumstances of the home's construction in his memoir, *Reminiscencias de una vida*, vol. 2 (Guadalajara, Mexico: Biblioteca de autores jaliscienses modernos, 1958), 53–57. The most detailed descriptions of Casa Zuno and its history can be found in essays by Avelino Sordo Vilchis, Cuauhtémoc de Regil, Arturo Camacho Becerrra, Gloria Becerra, and Javier Huízar Zuno in *La casa de tezontle: monografía de la casa Zuno* (Guadalajara, Mexico: Universidad de Guadalajara, 1998). See also Renato González Mello, "La casa Zuno, la casa González Luna," *Estudios jalicienses* 38 (November 1999): 7–23.

3. This type of figure has precedents in colonial palaces in Mexico City, such as the house of Conde de Heras Sota. See Manuel Toussaint, *Colonial Art in Mexico*, trans. and ed. Elizabeth Wilder Wesimann (Austin: University of Texas Press, 1967), 323, fig. 298.

4. Zuno, *Reminiscencias*, 53–54. Many of Zuno's ideas formed in the midst of the Mexican Revolution at the Centro Bohemio, an intellectual gathering founded by Zuno for young cultural leaders who discussed a wide array of topics, including politics, philosophy, social issues, and, notably, the social role of art. See Arturo Camacho Becerra, "Centro Bohemio de Guadalajara: arte y revolución (1912-1926)," in *Cultura y arte de gobernar en espacios y tiempos mexicanos*, eds. Nelly Sigaut and Thomas Calvo (Zamora, Mexico: El Colegio de Michoacán, 2015), 373–96.

5. Zuno, *Reminiscencias*, 54. All translations are by the author unless otherwise noted.

6. Mauricio Tenorio-Trillo, *Mexico at the World's Fairs: Crafting a Modern Nation* (Berkeley: University of California Press, 1996), 205–7; Enrique X. de Anda Alanís, *La arquitectura de la revolución mexicana: corrientes y estilos en la década de los veinte*, 2nd ed. (Mexico City: Instituto de Investigaciones Estéticas, Universidad Nacional Autónoma de Mexico, 2008), 131–36; Kathryn E. O'Rourke, *Modern Architecture in Mexico City: History, Representation, and the Shaping of a Capital* (Pittsburgh: University of Pittsburgh Press, 2016), 79–82.

7. De Anda Alanís, *La arquitectura de al revolución mexicana*, 136–57; O'Rourke, *Modern Architecture in Mexico City*, part 1, 25–147; Luis E. Carranza, "If Walls Could Talk: José Vasconcelos' *Raza Cósmica* and the Building for the Secretaría de Educación Pública," in *Architecture as Revolution: Episodes in the History of Modern Mexico* (Austin: University of Texas Press, 2010), 14–55.

8. Elsa Arroyo and Sandra Zetina, "The Reconstruction of Colonial Monuments in the 1920s and 1930s in Mexico," trans. Valerie Magar, *Conversaciones . . . con Nicholas Stanley-Price*, no. 9 (June 2020): 141–47.

9. Alicia Azuela, "Vasconcelos: educación y artes: un proyecto de cultura nacional," in *Antiguo Colegio de San Ildefenso*, 2nd ed., ed. Elisa Vargaslugo (Mexico City: Patronato del Antiguo Colegio de San Ildefenso, 1999), 143.

10. For discussions of this process, see Leonard Folgarait, *Mural Painting and Social Revolution in Mexico, 1920–1940: Art of the New Order* (Cambridge: Cambridge University Press, 1998), 16–20;

and Mary K. Coffey, "The 'Mexican Problem': Nation and 'Native' in Mexican Muralism and Cultural Discourse," in *The Social and the Real: Political Art of the 1930s in the Western Hemisphere*, eds. Alejandro Anreus, Diana L. Linden, and Jonathan Weinberg (University Park: The Pennsylvania State University Press, 2006), 46–50.

11. José Vasconcelos, *The Cosmic Race: A Bilingual Edition*, trans. Didier T. Jaén (Baltimore: The Johns Hopkins University Press, 1997), 16.

12. Ángel Rama, *The Lettered City*, trans. John Charles Chasteen (1984; Durham, NC: Duke University Press, 1996). Originally published as *La ciudad letrada* (Hanover, NH: Ediciones del Norte, 1984).

13. Carlos Monsiváis, quoted in Camacho Becerra, "Centro Bohemio de Guadalajara," 374. Originally published in Carlos Monsiváis, "Notas sobre la cultura mexicana en el siglo XX," in *Historia general de México*, vol. 4, eds. Berta Ulloa, Lorenzo Mayer, Jorge Alberto Manrique, and Carlos Monsiváis (Mexico City: Colegio de Mexico, 1976), http://www.jstor.com/stable/j.ctvt1shx5.7.

14. Jorge Alberto Manrique, "México se quiere otra vez barroco," in *Arquitectura neocolonial: América Latina, Caribe, Estados Unidos*, ed. Aracy A. Amaral (São Paulo: Memorial, Fonda de Cultura Económica, 1994), 40.

15. Carranza, "If Walls Could Talk," 32–34.

16. It is uncertain if the figures are Hernán Cortés and Moctezuma or Spaniard Nuño Beltrán de Guzmán, who spread the Conquest westward, and Tenamaxtli, the Caxcan leader.

17. Cristina López Uribe, "Mirror Gazes: Architecture in California and Mexico, 1915–1940," in *Found in Translation: Design in California and Mexico, 1915–1985*, ed. Wendy Kaplan (Los Angeles: Los Angeles County Museum of Art; DelMonico Books, 2017), 89.

18. James Oles, *Art and Architecture in Mexico* (New York: Thames & Hudson, 2013), 110–13.

19. Toussaint, *Colonial Art in Mexico*, 314–15.

20. Jacquelynn Bass, "*The Epic of American Civilization*: The Mural at Dartmouth College (1932–34)," in *José Clemente Orozco in the United States, 1927–34*, eds. Renato González Mello and Diane Miliotes (Hanover, NH: Hood Museum of Art, 2002), 165.

21. Zuno, *Reminiscencias*, 56–57. Leticia López Orozco attributes the doorframe paintings illustrated here to Guerrero in "Xavier Guerrero: motivos mexicanos," in *Muralismo mexicano 1920-1940: Catálogo razonado I*, ed. Ida Rodríguez Prampolini (Mexico City: Fondo de Cultura Económica, Universidad Veracruzana, Universidad Nacional Autónoma de México, Instituto Nacional de Bellas Artes y Literatura, 2012), 69, 70 (caption).

22. Lynda Klich, *The Noisemakers:* Estridentismo*, Vanguardism, and Social Action in Postrevolutionary Mexico* (Oakland: University of California Press, 2018), 59–63.

23. Olivier Debroise, *Figuras en el trópico, plástica mexicana 1920-1940* (Barcelona: Ediciones Océano, 1984), 37; Karen Cordero Reiman, "Constructing a Modern Mexican Art, 1910–1940," in *South of the Border: Mexico in the American Imagination, 1914–1947*, ed. James Oles (Washington, DC: Smithsonian Institution Press, 1993), 21. Cordero here designates the decorative style as the first "official art" of the postrevolutionary period.

24. Adrián Soto Villafaña, "Roberto Montenegro: El árbol de la vida, La danza de las horas or El árbol de la ciencia," in *Muralismo mexicano 1920-1940*, 12.

25. Julio Torri, "San Pedro y San Pablo," *Azulejos* 1, no. 7 (May 1922): 20.

26. Dr. Atl, *Las artes populares en México,* vol. 1 (Mexico City: Editorial Cultura, 1922), 135–36.

27. Camacho Becerra, "Centro Bohemio de Guadalajara," 387.

28. María de la Nieves Rodríguez, "La 'Noche Mexicana' como parte de los festejos de celebración de la Independencia de 1921," *Estudios* 105, no. 11 (Summer 2013): 63.

29. José Juan Tablada, "Mexican Painting of To-day," *International Studio* 76, no. 308 (January 1923): 274; Dr. Atl, *Las artes populares en México,* 53.

30. José Juan Tablada, "Arte mexicanista," *El Magazine de la raza* (September 1920). In Album de Carlos Mérida, Fondo Carlos Mérida, CENIDIAP, Mexico City, Rollo 11, no. 109.

31. Klich, *The Noisemakers*, 169–82.

32. Monserrat Sánchez Soler, ed. *Guillermo Ruiz y la Escuela de Escultura y Talla Directa* (Mexico City: Instituto Nacional de Bellas Artes, Consejo Nacional para la Cultura y las Artes, Museo Casa Estudio Diego Rivera y Frida Kahlo, 2010).

33. Zuno was a freemason, and González Mello has written about Casa Zuno in this regard in "La Casa Zuno, la casa González Luna," 11–14.

34. On Zuno's progressiveness, see Camacho Becerra, "Centro Bohemio de Guadalajara," 386.

35. Zuno, *Reminiscencias*, 55–56.

36. G[abriel] F[ernández] L[edesma], "Relieves de Juan Hernández," *Forma* 1 (October 1926): 35.

37. Zuno, *Reminiscencias*, 56; González Mello remarks on the tone of Zuno's language in "La Casa Zuno, la casa González Luna," 11.

38. Dr. Atl, "El pabellón de México en la Exposición de Rio de Janeiro," *Azulejos* 1, no. 6 (February 1922): 17.

39. Zuno, *Reminiscencias*, 57.

40. The manifesto, circulated as a broadsheet and published in the June 15–30 issue of *El Machete*, is translated by Tony Beckwith in *Inverted Utopias: Avant-garde Art in Latin America*, eds. Mari Carmen Ramírez and Héctor Olea (New Haven, CT: Yale University Press; Houston: The Museum of Fine Arts Houston), 461.

41. González Mello, "La casa Zuno, la casa González Luna," 12.

CRISTINA LÓPEZ URIBE

Antagonisms: Neocolonial vs. Functionalism in Mexico

This essay will analyze a complex moment of Mexican architectural history, contrasting two architectural expressions that were understood as opposites. The tension between contradictory poles—global and local, old and new, domestic and foreign—is part of the meaning of modernity writ large. In Mexico City in the 1930s, the differences between the variants of the Neocolonial, or architecture inspired by the Spanish precedent, were blurred with competing connotations. However, I will explore the different meanings that could be hiding under the totalizing stylistic designation of the Neocolonial style.[1]

Antagonisms

According to the anthropologist and journalist Anita Brenner, Federico Sánchez Fogarty was the man almost single-handedly responsible for the promotion of Functionalism in Mexico. In Esther Born's *The New Architecture in Mexico* (1937), the first book about modern architecture in Mexico, Brenner is quoted describing the success of the "smartly simple concrete and glass" of the "so-called 'functional'" architecture, that—according to her—was still a novelty almost everywhere except in Mexico where it was, by then, so completely familiar that it was taken for granted. "It is worth recording, with a smile, how that happened. First—the Tolteca Cement Company had concrete to sell and happened to command the services of an indefatigable and sophisticated advertising manager, Federico Sánchez Fogarty, who stormed the town with art contests, magazines, lectures, and all sorts of restless, intelligent pro-modern propaganda."[2]

Sánchez Fogarty was the editor of the cement company's magazine *Tolteca* (formerly named *Cemento*). In a later lecture, he explained he was having difficulty finding an editorial direction for the first issues, but then he learned about the "esthetics of construction" and "the revolution in architecture" taking place around the world from architects Manuel Ortiz Monasterio (1887–1967) and Bernardo Calderón Cabrera (1922–2003), who had designed La Nacional building. It was the first "tall" building in Mexico at thirteen stories, located across the street from the Bellas Artes Palace with its marble facade. To his surprise, the architects had left the concrete exposed as the finished surface.[3]

After spending full afternoons reading books by the Swiss architect Le Corbusier and journals with his friend Alberto Misrachi (a book seller who translated the texts from the French for him), he found the editorial direction that he was looking for. "In Le Corbusier I found the doctrine to save *Tolteca* from a fiasco. . . . I turned it from a simple bulletin as it was at the beginning, timid and smarmy, to an organ of a type of radical iconoclastic party although inexistent, but with a spear at the ready and willing, if necessary, to confront all the venerable plastic architecture of humanity's most glorious artistic past, to replace them with the new and absolute functionalist esthetics. . . . In short, for me, the esthetics of cement."[4]

His enthusiasm made him wish that the cathedral and, above all, the National Palace—which had a facade "not modern and not old"—would be substituted by buildings of the "new architectural era which was international and universal." Mr. Vivian—his boss—asked him to be careful with his words. After all, Hispanic symbols and images were still very popular, especially among the architects, the main readers of the magazine and the buyers of the product they were selling. Also, many powerful people, including the directors of the most important newspapers in those years, were from Spain.

"Fortunately," he explained, "and on time," his growing aversions to certain architectural styles ended up focusing on the Mexican version of the Spanish Colonial Revival style that emerged in Los Angeles County, California, but had nothing to do with Spain. He identified Hollywood as the origin place of the style, which was eventually transplanted to Mexico. His abhorrence reached its peak when Mr. Vivian sent him to Los Angeles. He wrote an article in 1931, "The Farce of Los Angeles," that became popular and was published in several outlets. Sánchez Fogarty lamented that he was never able to write so eloquently in favor of European Functionalism as he was able to write against the touristic esthetics of southern California.[5]

In this amusing article, he narrated his surprise at finding buildings that looked like old churches but were oil warehouses, temples that were gas stations, gardens disguised like patios, and fake concrete ruins of a pretend ancient architecture from the Padres. He described Los Angeles as "the most fake city in the world." This was perhaps the first use of the pejorative term "colonial *californiano*" to denote architecture that artificially recreated the viceregal past. "In Los Angeles nothing is true," repeated Sánchez Fogarty throughout the article. "Now, every time I see in Mexico a colonial californiano style house my spirit is disturbed. It is bad, very bad that in Los Angeles they slavishly, grotesquely, extemporaneously, imitate in their modern constructions the glorious colonial styles of Mexico; but it will be worse if we in Mexico continue importing this false and Hollywoodesque style."[6]

When Sánchez Fogarty came back from LA, which he called jokingly "Spainland" (*Españolandia*), and saw the new cement plant in Mixcoac "bare of ornaments," he had the idea of organizing an art competition—the Tolteca competition of 1931—to promote the "new era." The goal was to inspire painters, illustrators, and photographers with the company's functional buildings. He wanted the factory to be a source of inspiration for new generations of architects

CASA HABITACION

Por MAURICIO GOMEZ MAYORGA

Fig. 1. Mauricio Gómez Mayorga (text and drawings), "Casa habitación," *Arquitectura México* 7 (April 1941): 54–55. Archivo Histórico FA UNAM.

and for them to join the vigorous personalities that already were working "to stop the advance of the fake Angelino style," which included Manuel Ortiz Monasterio, Carlos Obregón Santacilia (1896–1961), Vicente Mendiola (1900–1986), and Juan O'Gorman (1905–1982).[7]

With Sánchez Fogarty's writings and activities, the promotion of Functionalism and the criticism of Colonial Californiano started simultaneously. His selection of names is interesting since three of the four architects mentioned had worked in the Neocolonial style (Juan O'Gorman was the exception), and one of them, Obregón Santacilia, was the main architect of the official Neocolonial style as formulated a decade earlier and supported by the cultural elite of the immediate postrevolutionary state. Obregón Santacilia was still designing neocolonial structures at the time; however, he also strongly promoted Functionalism, for example, by organizing in 1932 a competition to design workers' housing.

What concrete could and couldn't be used for was still not entirely settled. Between 1924 and 1930, businesses promoted the use of concrete for neocolonial buildings and motifs, but after 1931, the advertising of cement shifted to functionalist architecture, emphasizing what Sánchez Fogarty called the esthetics of cement. The issues of *Cemento* make clear, though, that the aesthetics of cement were also Spanish since much of the revolution in the construction industry and building materials was actually carried out in the realm of the Neocolonial style, and those buildings were highly publicized in the advertising campaigns as concrete structures.[8]

By the middle of the 1930s, modernist structures inundated the city. However, neocolonial buildings and colonial californiano structures, in all price ranges, from very small ones in the lower-income neighborhoods of Narvarte or Portales and the middle-class developments of Hipódromo de la Condesa and Colonia del Valle

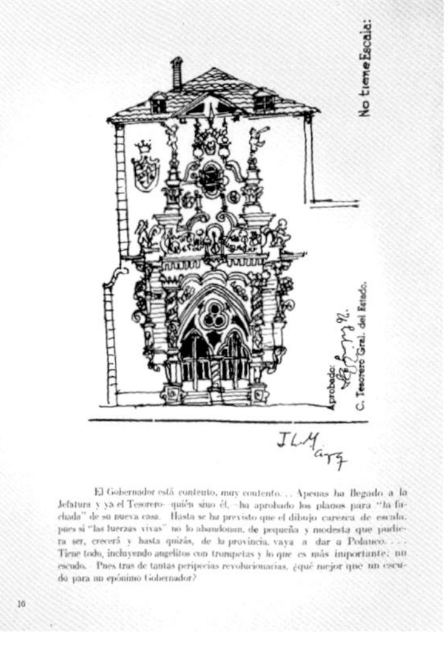

Fig. 2. Jorge L. Medellín, untitled cartoon in *Arquitectura y lo demás* 1 (May 1945): 10. Archivo Histórico FA UNAM.

Fig. 3. Jorge L. Medellín or Gómez Rosas, "Pan de muertos o de 'Vivos'?" *Arquitectura y lo demás* 6 (October–November 1945): 50. Archivo Histórico FA UNAM.

to the biggest and most expensive in the Polanco neighborhood and Chapultepec Heights (now Lomas de Chapultepec), still thrived.

Short stories making fun of the nightmares of owning a "colonial house"—which had, according to the architects, very unpractical solutions for modern life—were common in architectural magazines in the 1930s, especially in the functionalist ones, such as *Edificación*, the magazine of the technical school of architecture founded by O'Gorman and others in 1932.[9] In one article, O'Gorman declared traditionalist architecture defeated in a technical knockout by the prefabricated houses of American Houses Inc.; however, it wasn't beaten.[10] A decade later, these kinds of criticisms appeared even in the more conservative magazines, such as Mario Pani's *Arquitectura México* (fig.1).[11]

Satirical drawings and stories continued throughout World War II in *Arquitectura México* and especially after the war in *Arquitectura y lo demás*, whose first issue included a satirical sketch, announcing one of its many enemies.[12] Architect Jorge L. Medellín's cartoon made fun of a new governor who was very happy about the new facade of his house: "It has everything, including little angels with trumpets and what is more important: a coat of arms. After so many revolutionary skills what better than a coat of arms for an eponymous governor?" the article wondered (fig. 2). The drawing had no graphic scale because "as small and modest as it might be, it will grow and perhaps even end up in Polanco from the province."[13]

In the second issue of the magazine, another satirical illustration by architect Raul Cacho accompanied the news of new building regulations in the city that now required a degree. He portrayed "the architect's sin": "To be daydreaming (on the clouds) while the opportunists (*vivos*), engineers, contractors and other charlatans, exploited people with Colonial Californiano style little houses under the protection of the law."[14] These critical architects disregarded the fact that many of those houses were designed by well-regarded architects and engineers, such as Francisco J. Serrano (1900–1982).

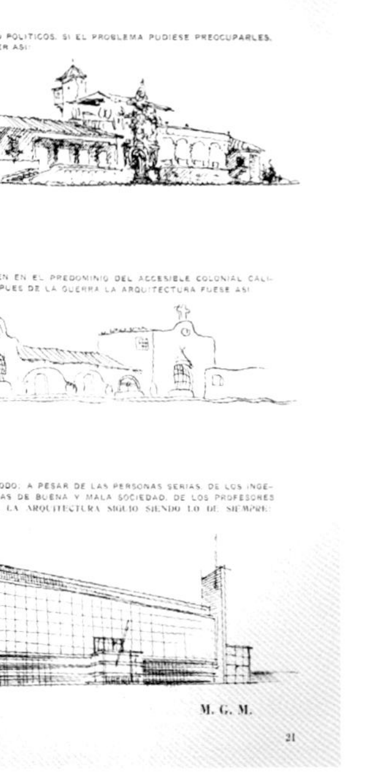

Fig. 4. Mauricio Gómez Mayorga, "Las personas serias pensaron . . . ," *Arquitectura y lo demás* 9 (April–August 1946): 21. Archivo Histórico FA UNAM.

The sixth issue was the most creative: it included an insert of several pages of colored tissue paper, simulating flyers common on the celebrations of Day of the Dead. It started with a drawing by Medellín and Gómez Rosas showing a colonial californiano house on the top of a traditional *pan de muertos* (bread of the dead) and several skulls around it. Above and below, it reads "Pan de muertos . . . o de '*Vivos*'?"— "the bread of the dead or the opportunists'?" (fig. 3). It was followed by several literary *calaveras*, traditional sarcastic verses, also part of the Day of the Dead celebration, that made fun of the Californian provenance of the style now so popular in Mexico.[15]

In Mauricio Gómez Mayorga's drawings in the ninth issue, he muses about the stylistic expectations of people after World War II. The capitalists and politicians prefer large, baroque colonial californiano homes, while families prefer more modest and accessible versions. But in the end, Gómez Mayorga finishes with a drawing of glass-and-steel functionalist structure and declares: "In spite of it all . . . architecture will continue to be architecture" (fig. 4).[16]

Judging by these types of critiques, both styles represented two antagonistic ways of understanding architecture. If we see the history of architecture as an evolutionary trajectory toward abstract modern architecture, unadorned, without references to the past, it is inevitable that we think—as the protagonists did in the 1950s—that the Neocolonial, in broad terms, was a necessary first step to put an end to academic Beaux-Arts training but eventually needed to be left behind.[17] However, this vision is not entirely correct since, with few exceptions, Hispanic motifs have always been, and continue to be, present in Mexican modern architecture, not only in anonymous, commercial architecture but also in buildings by the most prominent architects, such as Luis Barragán (1902–1988).

We might even say that the winner of the battle between the styles was, in fact, the Neocolonial, and the loser was Functionalism, at least the radical version championed by O'Gorman, Juan Legarreta (1902–1934), and Álvaro Aburto (1905–1976), which was considered by many not adequate for Mexican soil.[18]

During the series of conferences organized by the Society of Mexican Architects, later published as *Pláticas sobre arquitectura 1933*, most of the architects thought that the styles from the viceregal period could (and should) not be imitated but were aware that the clients still "demanded their house in colonial, Californian or German [meaning functionalist] style." For that reason, which was the stated purpose of organizing the conferences, they wanted to find an architectural expression that suited the Mexican reality: its social customs, weather, and local materials, each of which was "very different from those which existed in other countries at other times, very different also of the one that existed in Mexico in the viceregal era, or, not going so far back, in the years before the revolution."[19] However, on the one hand, most of the architects were not happy with Neocolonial's functional alternative which removed the search for beauty from the architect's duty. Significantly, O'Gorman's defense of Functionalism disregarded all stylistic considerations as "spiritual needs," not as imperative as material ones.[20] In arguing against art for art's sake, O'Gorman labeled all historical inspiration "artistic archaeology."[21] On the other hand, the stronger accusations against Functionalism were about its European origin, especially the large windows "imported directly from Scandinavia, and of such magnitudes as to catch the pale glares of the midnight sun and the diffused light, which in those countries distribute with dropper" but that needed heavy curtains to adapt to "our blue skies and tropical light."[22]

Fig. 5. Vicente Mendiola, Plutarco Elías Calles house, Anzures, Mexico City, 1933. Arch. V. Mendiola Family Archive.

Antagonism?

In spite of all of this, and the obvious contradictory positions between using tradition and the avant-garde's break with the past, we can find some points of union between these architectural approaches.

While the postrevolutionary presidents supported radical Functionalism for public works—O'Gorman's primary schools and Legarreta's settlements for workers—for their own houses, they preferred the Neocolonial. In 1933, former president Plutarco Elías Calles hired architect Vicente Mendiola to design his home in Anzures near the presidential residence at the Chapultepec Castle while he continued to control the country during the historical period known as Maximato (1928–34). Mendiola designed an elegant mansion with some Art Deco motifs but with an unquestionable Hispanic atmosphere (fig. 5). He also hired Obregón Santacilia to design his home in Cuernavaca, the Quinta Las Palmas (1932), where a huge window with wrought-iron grilles and a quadrangular tower covered in red tiles were the protagonists and visually controlled the landscape (fig. 6). While both architects were famous for their neocolonial work and were well-respected among the guild of architects, their more modest domestic architectures read more as Colonial Californiano.[23] In the same year, Obregón Santacilia also designed the house for Calles's neighbor and business partner, Federico T. de Lachica, who was in the steel business

Fig. 6. Carlos Obregón Santacilia, Working design drawing for Plutarco Elías Calles house, Cuernavaca, 1932. Fototeca / Planoteca de la Dirección de Arquitectura y Conservación del Patrimonio Artístico Inmueble DACPAI-INBAL.

and worked as a contractor for the government with his company Fomento y Urbanización S. A. (FYUSA; fig. 7). Together with a third house owned by Aaron Sáenz Garza—governor of the Federal District from 1932 to 1935, a powerful politician, and a business associate of FYUSA—the houses formed part of a Spanish fantasy land where vital State decisions happened near a golf club and a park, the Revolution Park, designed in the same style by Mendiola.[24]

The next president, Lázaro Cárdenas, also favored modernism for the construction of schools, hospitals, and government buildings but lived in "country" houses, or *casas de pueblo*, that recreated the viceregal past.[25] Paradoxically, Cárdenas asked radical functionalist architect Álvaro Aburto to create building regulations in the late 1930s to preserve the traditional, colonial character of Michoacán's small towns, in part to promote tourism. His designs of predefined traditional windows, grilles, railings, roofs, etc., and the prohibition of commercial hardware ran counter to how the functionalist architect usually worked.[26] Aburto also designed houses for peasants that looked similar to vernacular architecture, some of them with Obregón Santacilia, using an experimental prefabricated building technique.[27]

Functionalist ideals like honesty and authenticity and the desire to break with anything related to academic training had points in common with already existing anonymous and vernacular architecture that had been created to fulfill a specific need with no greater aspirations. The houses designed by Obregón Santacilia in 1926

Fig. 7. Carlos Obregón Santacilia, Federico T. de Lachica house, Cuernavaca, 1932. Presentation drawing by the construction company Fomento y Urbanización S. A. Fototeca / Planoteca DACPAI-INBAL.

and described by Diego Rivera as the "neighborhood house of cheap apartments, hygienic and beautiful" had already used concepts associated with functionalist architecture. For example, Obregón Santacilia "avoided all camouflage, all waste of material, employing as factors of beauty the economy of materials and their maximum utility."[28] The search for simplicity and purity, the movement toward abstraction, the roughness of textures, and the arrangement of functional things from the past can be found in both neocolonial and modern functional structures.[29]

But the irregularity, roughness, and asymmetry of the colonial californiano buildings highlighted romantic notions. Some scholars have connected this with the aesthetic principle of the picturesque in the Arts & Crafts movement, which Mexican architects saw in American books and journals.[30] However, ornaments were not problematic from a structural perspective, and the use of baroque ornament allowed design liberties without interfering with structural sincerity. It was an architecture that allowed future adaptations. In many ways, the neocolonial structures could be interpreted as "an unusual version of functionalism."[31]

All of the functionalist architects studied carefully the old colonial buildings. O'Gorman supervised the detailed drawings of civil colonial buildings and *vecindades*. His family home was a full Spanish colonial fantasy, his father—originally from Ireland—was a mining engineer and a painter who collected colonial antiques from old churches and hired carpenters known for their neocolonial furniture designs. He even dressed up like a monk and designed some colonial-inspired furnishings for his home.

Like the other functionalist architects (Legarreta, Aburto, Fernández), O'Gorman was part of a commission led by the prominent researcher Manuel Toussaint to study the picturesque town of Taxco to be promoted as a tourist destination but also to boost appreciation of the old monuments tied to the town's traditional character.[32] Talented architects like Mendiola were very important for the rebuilding of viceregal structures lost in earthquakes, war, and other tragic events. However, substitution opened the path to fantasy and exaggeration, and nowadays, it is difficult to distinguish what was built in the Neocolonial style and what constitutes an original viceregal building. In an article in *Arquitectura México*, Toussaint complained that the Church of Coyoacán was "pitifully destroyed to build a temple in Colonial Californiano style."[33]

The appreciation and defense of the old Spanish colonial buildings did not automatically confer approval of the Neocolonial style. In contrast to President Calles, Toussaint, a former member of the Ateneo de la Juventud

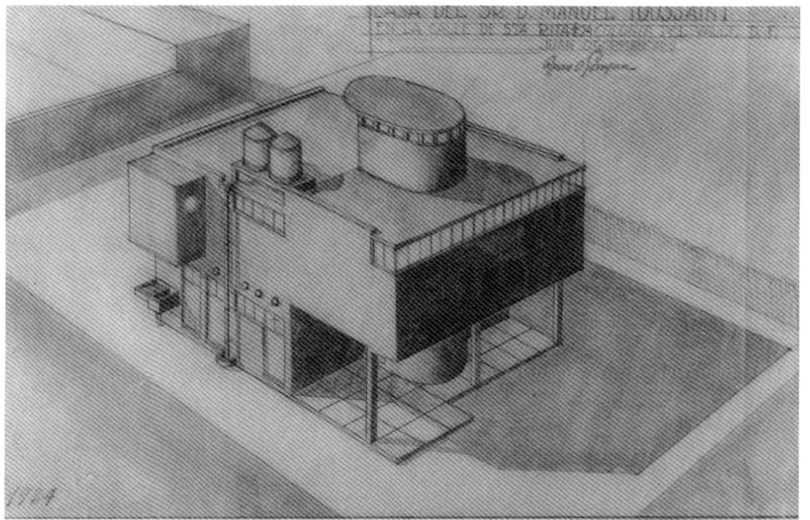

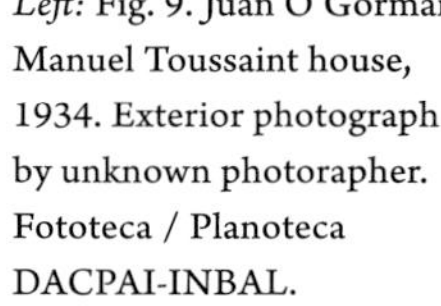

Above: Fig. 8. Juan O'Gorman, Manuel Toussaint house, 1934. Isometric drawing. Fototeca / Planoteca DACPAI-INBAL.

Left: Fig. 9. Juan O'Gorman, Manuel Toussaint house, 1934. Exterior photograph by unknown photorapher. Fototeca / Planoteca DACPAI-INBAL.

Right: Fig. 10. Juan O'Gorman, Manuel Toussaint house, 1934. Exterior photograph by unknown photographer. Fototeca / Planoteca DACPAI-INBAL.

Far right: Fig. 11. Juan O'Gorman, Manuel Toussaint house, 1934. Interior photograph showing Toussaint's studio by unknown photographer. Fototeca / Planoteca DACPAI-INBAL.

(a cultural association that formulated Mexican nationalism), decided to live in one of the most radical house designs by O'Gorman (figs. 8–10). Eclipsed by the notoriety of the studios for Diego Rivera and Frida Kahlo, the other houses designed by O'Gorman in the 1930s deserve a full study. Toussaint's house in the Colonia del Valle neighborhood of Mexico City is a small building in the center of the plot with a cantilevered second floor that creates a covered terrace. The main facade features a high horizontal window that runs the entire length of the wall belonging to the library-study that occupies half of the second floor. The interior staircase is cylindrical and sticks out above the flat roof, and there are no parapets of any kind. There is no reference to colonial times here, in the house of the most important defender of viceregal architecture. Only the wooden chair could be considered a reminder of the Hispanic past (fig. 11).[34]

Spanish Paradox

The search for something called "National Architecture" was an international phenomenon at the turn of the century. In Mexico, the idea that an authentic national architecture could exist and that it should be related to the colonial period had been proposed since 1901 and was common to other Latin American countries. But the official Mexican version of the Neocolonial was to a large degree developed and fabricated by the young intellectuals and artists gathered at the Ateneo de la Juventud, a Mexican *bohème* of the turn of the century. The group wanted to renovate the country's cultural world before and during the Mexican Revolution, and its members proved to be instrumental in the postrevolutionary period when the nation needed to fabricate a positive self-image. One of them was the famous Jose Vasconcelos, a strong supporter—for some, imposer—of the Neocolonial style in the first postrevolutionary public buildings.

The architect Jesús T. Acevedo (1882–1918) organized evening gatherings with his friends from the Ateneo where they read the classics and posed like characters from Velázquez paintings. He was credited with inventing the idea of the Neocolonial in his 1914 lectures, published as a posthumous book by his friend Federico Mariscal in 1920.[35] Fascinated with gothic cathedrals and a reader of John Ruskin, Acevedo agreed with Oscar Wilde that the Gothic "was not allowed to develop on its own lines, but was interrupted and spoiled by the dreary classical Renaissance." Since then, architecture has no longer been considered important by the people.[36] With his words, we can picture the romantic scene and mindset when the idea of the Neocolonial was born:

Nothing more pleasant for my spirit, than the silent evocation that swiftly traverses the desert of my memories, transports me to the mornings of my student life, when, together with a group of cheerful and ardent companions like a flock of free sparrows, I conversed with them about our native architecture. Then, as we had the terraces of the old Academy at our discretion, we spent a good part of the day there contemplating one by one—and sometimes drawing them—all the towers and domes of the religious monuments that the Spanish domination built on our land. And no terrestrial spectacle had, to the delight of our eyes, the truly suggestive charm that the metropolis offered us, rich in lanterns decorated with tiles, when they burned, shimmering under the thousand golden arrows of the morning sun. . . . And in that city labyrinth that stretched ashen as far as the eye could see, the unique colonial monuments triumphed for the decisive curves of their domes, for the undulating profiles of their gabled walls, for their finials, spherical caps and bell towers that inscribed in the serene sky, its many vigorous and determined contours![37]

He believed that Mexican colonial architecture—just like gothic architecture—was also interrupted, which was a shame because it could have evolved to adapt to modern times: "That way we could now have a style to call our own."[38]

While many architects turned toward Indigenous examples during this time, Acevedo thought Indigenous American architecture was only good for archaeological wonderings; according to him, nothing about it could contribute to a movement of transcendental importance. Despite these pronouncements, the success of the Neocolonial rested on the integration of Indigenous and Hispanic. Acevedo put it in these terms: "When the natives translated with admirable dedication the foreign strokes that served as their model, something native and remote hid in their work. Something unknown and profound, that without mistaking dimensions or deviating from the guidelines, nevertheless put a new gesture, an unexpected nuance, a special color; in short, it was our Mexico that pointed out its idiosyncrasy." Acevedo saw that "in the implantation of any style and any architectural tendency by the conquerors, both are modified by a 'dark trend' always present in the natives." That the imposed architectural styles somehow always remain local is "due to that secret and formidable opposition of every civilization towards any imposed civilization."[39]

It was equally clear for Acevedo that Spain could not teach any pure styles because it imported them all. "I wonder if our colonial style,

EL PABELLÓN D MÉXICO EN LA EXPOSICIÓN D RÍO D JANEIRO

ARTÍCULO D EL DR. ATL

La Secretaría de Industria y Comercio abrió un concurso para un pabellón de México en la exposición de Río de Janeiro.

Concurrieron 9 arquitectos. El jurado calificador otorgó el premio a los jóvenes Carlos Obregón Santacilia y Carlos H. Tarditi.

El proyecto, de estilo colonial es, seguramente, una de las tentativas mejor logradas para crear un estilo neo-colonial, es decir, una arquitectura propiamente mexicana.

He podido ver en los talleres de Obregón y Tarditi el desarrollo del proyecto premiado, y puedo asegurar que la construcción de este edificio será la primera manifestación *decente* y bella de la arquitectura nacional en el extranjero.

Hasta ahora esta clase de construcciones había sido encomendada a ingenieros ignorantes de la arquitectura o arquitectos salidos de las páginas manoseadas de los libracos de la Boblioteca de la Escuela Nacional de Bellas Artes. Los pabellones de las exposiciones de San Luis y de París fueron, bajo todos conceptos, vergonzosas imposiciones de la cretinería oficial.

Hoy la Secretaría de Industria y Comercio ha comprendido la importancia de la participación mexicana en las exposiciones extranjeras y ha creído necesario organizar dignamente las exhibiciones nacionales. Ya en Dallas llevó a cabo una exposición importante, y, gracias a su iniciativa, México podrá tener en Río de Janeiro un pabellón que será sin duda alguna entre los más bellos que se levanten en la gran feria de la capital del Brasil.

El proyecto de Obregón-Tarditi corresponde perfectamente a las necesidades indicadas en la convocatoria y a las exigencias de un pabellón de exposiciones.

La planta del edificio es una planta colonial, es decir la construcción se desarrolla al derredor de un patio.

La arquitectura mexicana a la que se ha puesto el nombre de *arquitectura colonial*, es una resultante de muy diversos factores y no solamente del criterio estético español, como hasta la fecha se ha afirmado. Hay en ella elementos de origen italiano, especialmente en las construcciones de los religiosos franciscanos y en la disposición de algunas mansiones señoriales; existen en abundancia los elementos torturados de Churriguera, las transformaciones múltiples del plateresco, y, desde el punto de vista exclusivamente técnico, es de suma importancia la influencia constante de la habilidad y del sentimiento de los obreros indígenas que construyeron las iglesias, los palacios, las casas y los monumentos votivos que forman la genuina representación del arte colonial.

Todos estos factores dan a la arquitectura colonial un carácter bizarro, pintoresco, osado. La arquitectura colonial es una arquitectura revolucionaria. Ha roto con todos los moldes, con todo el clasicismo y es, especialmente en las iglesias, básicamente ornamental.

Las condiciones climatéricas de México, la calidad de los materiales de construcción, la baratura de la mano de obra, permitieron a los constructores coloniales levantar en el espacio de dos siglos y medio una obra que en su conjunto es de una variedad extraordinaria y que, desde el punto de vista de la cantidad, es siempre superior a lo que muchas civilizaciones han construido en periodos de tiempo más largos.

Ningún estilo arquitectónico post-azteca corresponde mejor, ni representa mejor, al sentimiento artístico mexicano como el estilo colonial.

No es pués extraño que los arquitectos modernos en México se inspiren en las construcciones de este estilo

17

Fig. 12. Dr. Atl, "El pabellón de México en la Exposicion de Río de Janeiro," *Azulejos* 6 (February 1922): 17. Biblioteca Manuel Toussaint, IIE UNAM.

Fig. 13. Carlos Obregón Santacilia and Carlos Tarditi (under the pseudonym Rodrigo de Pontecillos), proposal for the main facade of the Mexican Pavilion at the Exposition of Rio de Janeiro, 1921. Watercolor on paper. Fototeca / Planoteca DACPAI-INBAL.

made of fragments, could in turn constitute an exemplary style; if its study should be an indispensable discipline and if, despite the change in customs since the beginning of the nineteenth century, it could be a matter of evolution and finally of current application." He and his generation especially loved the Sagrario Metropolitano next to the cathedral; as he said, "We have the right to proclaim national this art made of hidden reason and lavish wealth."[40]

The idea was not to master an architectural style of the past but to exercise it and evolve it into a modern expression. It was Mariscal, Acevedo's friend and professor of architecture at the San Carlos Academy, who most promoted the study and protection of viceregal monuments threatened with destruction. He also applied the idea of *mestizaje* to architecture's role in forming the country's identity. According to him, Mexican architecture should be based on the one that emerged and developed when "the Mexican [essence] was constituted" during the three centuries that New Spain lasted.[41]

All these ideas—developed during the revolution—took on different meanings after the end of the war with the construction of the nation's new international image and a Mexican identity for its people. Just as the artists and painters were revolutionizing art, organizing folk art exhibitions and painting the walls of the old colonial buildings, architects needed a revolution of their own, so the most audacious young architects, as a way to rebel against their academic training, started to experiment in the search of a new colonial style.

In a 1922 article, Dr. Atl—one of the revolutionary artists—presented the winning proposal for the Mexican pavilion at the centennial exposition in Rio de Janeiro by architects Obregón Santacilia and Carlos Tarditi (1894–1947) as "one of the best attempts to create a neo-colonial style," perhaps the first use of that term. "This will be the first decent and beautiful manifestation of our National architecture abroad," he said. After explaining the multiple style references from Europe, he added, "and exclusively from the technical point of view, it is very important the constant influence of the native workers who were the ones that built the monuments. All this combination gave the colonial architecture a bizarre painteresque, daring personality. The colonial architecture is a revolutionary architecture. It has broken all the molds, all classicism." For Dr. Atl, it was only natural that a true artistic renovation would be inspired in this style (figs. 12–13).[42]

Around the same time, Alfonso Pallares, the president of the Society of Mexican Architects, believed that neoclassical architecture—the predominant style of the nineteenth century—was an artificial convention born of repetition because it did not come from direct observation of reality. The search for the solution of the architectural quests by drawing in the atelier was one of the causes of its decadence. The reason why Mexico did not have a national architecture was because Spanish architects during the viceregal era brought an art already based in this artificiality: they were merely copying the buildings from books. However,

> *there were the monuments . . . to tell us that when Mexican architects did not know about the laws of the classic orders, or the laws of the Romanic, or the Gothic, or the Renaissance . . . they created architectonic vocabularies of very powerful originality and indisputable architectural value. . . . The aboriginal ideology is anti-Greek, and the molds in which our architectural conception is to be cast are taken from Greek ideology. There lies the essential mistake. It will be said that we are not Indians, but apart from the fact that the majority Republic's population is indigenous, the mestizo people by their origin, by their environment, by the influence of the nature where they have emerged, despite having modified the aboriginal ideology by education and the influence of the Spanish civilization, they are still actually absolutely strange to Greek psychology.*[43]

Both Dr. Atl and Pallares laid out that the guiding principles of a national architecture were not to be found in what the Spanish colonial carried from Spain or from Europe but in what it had from Mexico: its adaptation—a mestizaje of races and a mestizaje of styles. These concepts were an invention, an oversimplification, but they proved useful.

The Mexican pavilion in Rio constituted for Dr. Atl "an evolution of colonial art untied to any architectural prejudice Italian, French or classic." He summarized the pavilion as "the colonial ornamental spirit organized with greater logic in a very solid structure."[44] His choice of words is striking, considering that the pavilion was actually built in wood and plaster: an extremely rare solution for any Mexican structure but one that was common in the context of international exhibitions (fig. 14).

The uniqueness of the Neocolonial style, then, rested in ornament. Importantly, the ornament was created on Mexican soil. It was a Mexican product, and a modern one. Dr. Atl's reference to Mexican soil seems curious since the building was not designed for Mexican soil but for Rio de Janeiro. Dr. Atl had a hidden intention. The pavilion design was Mexican in its opposition to Spanish Colonial Revival as

Fig. 14. Carlos Obregón Santacilia and Carlos Tarditi, architectural drawings of the central "altarpiece" of the main facade in plaster and wood, Mexican Pavilion at the Exhibition of Rio de Janeiro, 1922. Fototeca / Planoteca DACPAI-INBAL.

Left: Fig. 15. Francisco J. Serrano, architectural drawing for Raul Basurto house, Hipódromo de la Condesa, 1936. Acervo de Arquitectura Mexicana FA UNAM, fondo Francisco J. Serrano.

Right: Fig. 16. Francisco J. Serrano, presentation drawing for Guadalupe building, Emilio Castelar 6, Polanco, 1939. Acervo de Arquitectura Mexicana FA UNAM, fondo Francisco J. Serrano.

formulated in the United States, what would come to be derided as Colonial Californiano. For Dr. Atl, American architects were merely copying colonial monuments, as he saw evident at San Diego's Panama-California Exposition of 1915.

American Paradox

Spanish-Colonial Architecture in Mexico, written by the Bostonian Sylvester Baxter, was one of the first works to promote the appreciation of viceregal buildings in Mexico. Baxter traveled throughout the country by train at the turn of the century, accompanied by the young architect Bertram Goodhue (1869–1924).[45] Goodhue later designed the buildings for the San Diego Panama-California Exposition of 1915 that were a milestone for Californian architects, signaling the style that could represent the region: Spanish Colonial Revival. The extreme popularity of this style transcended the architectural world. Images of the region's Spanish past were already very popular in literature. Fueled by the fantasy of lost exotic lands, the tourist industry exploited such images to promote travel to the South and, when the Mexican Revolution was over, across the border. The Hollywood movie industry spread Spanish colonial images around the world. For many years, Europeans' image of America, and especially Latin America, relied on early westerns.[46]

Like many other Americans, Santa Barbara's prominent architects George Washington Smith (1876–1930) and Lutah Maria Riggs (1896–1984) traveled to Mexico in 1922, while Dr. Atl was celebrating the Mexican Pavilion in Rio. Riggs made numerous drawings and photographs documenting everything she saw—doors, stairs, railings, from the humblest houses to the most elaborate churches—in order to reproduce them in their Santa Barbara houses. Their houses were frequently published in architectural magazines that Mexican architects, like Francisco J. Serrano, kept in their studios.

All revitalization requires knowledge of the source, so publications and photography were vital to this project. Architects created photographic collections of ornamental details to use as a catalogue of forms for their later building projects. American books and journals served as manuals to a generation of architects. Serrano's collection of magazines explains his stylistic tastes. He owned issues of *House & Garden*, *The House Beautiful*, *Good Furniture and Decoration*, *Arts and Decoration* (the French and the US versions), *The Architectural Forum*, *Moderne Bauformen*, *The*

American Architect, and *Architecture*, and many of these issues have bookmarks. Through this collection, we can see where he found inspiration for his houses that ranged from Art Deco and Colonial Californiano style to Modernism with some traces of German Expressionism.

Serrano worked for the real estate development company De la Lama y Basurto S. A., designing model houses for new neighborhoods. He was asked by the developers in 1931 to design most of them in the Colonial Californiano style because of the style's popularity.[47] These were small houses, designed to be bought on easy installments, that drew from US mass-media images but deviated from the Spanish colonial revival examples. Serrano's innovation of the domestic space incorporated rooms that were common in US architecture but that were not found in Mexican houses, such as the nook, the pantry, and the garage, which he labeled in English on his drawings. Instead of the traditional patio of colonial houses or other Beaux-Art style layouts, a central hall, sometimes two stories, was popular at the time (fig. 15). Additionally, unlike traditional houses, the new houses were set in the middle of the plot and surrounded by a garden—though often smaller than US examples, not unlike O'Gorman's functionalist designs of the same years. Serrano used the same architectural language to redesign the home of the development's owner, Raul Basurto, in the Condesa neighborhood, originally designed by Mendiola in the Art Deco style (fig. 16).

In the wealthy neighborhood of Polanco, the same real estate company required that the buildings in the center of the development comply with the neocolonial atmosphere, and Serrano's Pasaje Polanco (1938) is the best example. The four-story building includes apartments, shops on the ground floor, and an interior street that articulates the urban vitality of the neighborhood, and he skillfully designed every piece of urban furniture. Serrano also experimented with other complicated, multipurpose, and multistoried structures, like the Guadalupe building (1939), in an attempt to elaborate the style outside the single-family domestic realm (fig. 17). Mexican Colonial Californiano proved so successful that it was exported to other countries as the "Mexican style," but it also carried with it the pejorative connotations it had among Mexican architects because of its associations with the US. Because of this rejection and disregard of the style by historians, it has not been much studied.[48]

A Delicate Balance

Besides the associations with the US, the style also carried more obvious connotations. With its white stuccoed walls, baroque stone details, arches, and red tile roofs, these houses clearly evoked the provenance of a country where many still had strong ties and considered the motherland. People from Spain were still very powerful in the country, including the most important newspaper publishers. Spain was still strongly invested in

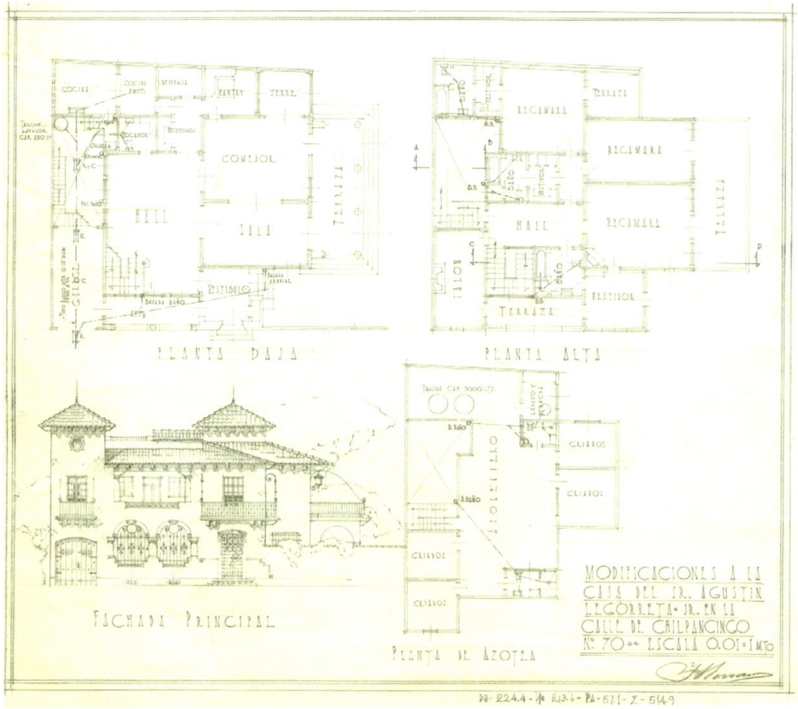

Fig. 17. Francisco J. Serrano, architectural drawing for Agustín Legorreta house, Hipódromo de la Condesa, undated. Acervo de Arquitectura Mexicana FA UNAM, fondo Francisco J. Serrano.

projecting an image of a unified country during the dictatorship of Miguel Primo de Rivera (1923–30) and cultivating the perception of its control over the Latin American countries, as exemplified in the Ibero-American Exhibition, held in Seville in 1929.

Despite these more international connotations, the colonial californiano houses also echoed and romanticized the Mexican vernacular and the countryside in the urban metropolis. A better explanation of its popularity can be found in the images and arguments originating in the Mexican Revolution. It made sense that postrevolutionary politics would draw from the sources that symbolized the countryside at a moment when the revolutionaries were fulfilling promises made to the peasant-soldiers who fought in the civil war. Similarly, Ranchero movies, such as *Allá en el rancho grande* by Fernando de Fuentes, romanticized rural life and reached huge international success in the late 1930s and 1940s.

Colonial californiano houses can be understood as perfectly designed artifacts that ambiguously symbolized both the countryside and the modern life of the metropolis and were at once perceived as delicately balancing the American and the Spanish. The US influence in Mexico frequently influenced the debates between those who supported Spain and those who resented the presence and power that the Spaniards still had in Mexico. Many believed that the only defense against the danger of the expansion of the US was strengthening their Spanish culture. The idea that the anti-Spanish sentiment could be interpreted as a pro-US affiliation was latent.[49] In this context, perhaps one of the reasons for Colonial Californiano's popularity with politicians and foreigners was that they were able to sidestep favoring one foreign power over the other in the confusing cultural scene of Mexico in the 1930s. In the following decades, a national, cosmopolitan Mexican modernism was formulated that displaced the contested Functionalism.

Notes

1. "It is well known that totalizing stylistic designations tend to become obstacles to research, imposing unifying criteria or general definitions where flexibility and conceptual breadth are needed to advance new ideas." Pancho Liernur, "¿Arquitectura del imperio español o arquitectura criolla? Notas sobre las representaciones 'neocoloniales' de la arquitectura producida durante la dominación española en la América," *Anales del Instituto de Arte Americano e Investigaciones Estéticas "Mario J. Buschiazzo"* 27–28 (1989–91): 208.

2. Anita Brenner, *Your Mexican Holiday: A Modern Guide* (New York: G. P. Putman's Sons, 1935), 110, quoted in Esther Born, *The New Architecture in Mexico* (New York: William Morrow & Co., Architectural Record, 1937), 12, first published in *Architectural Record* 81, no. 4 (April 1937): 12.

3. Conference presented April 4–10, 1937, organized by the National Association of Publicists at the Ateneo Nacional de Artes y Ciencias de México. Published as Federico Sánchez Fogarty, "Publicidad institucional," *Edificación* 4, no. 3 (March–April 1937): 26–31, 29. All translations from Spanish are by the author.

4. Ibid., 29.

5. Ibid., 30. "The Farce of Los Angeles" was originally published in *Excélsior*, September 1, 1931:14. It was republished in *Síntesis* (October 1931): 123–25 and *Tolteca* 21 (January 1932): 301–4.

6. Federico Sánchez Fogarty, "La farsa de Los Ángeles," *Tolteca* 21 (January 1931): 303. Originally published in *Excelsior*, September 1, 1931, 14.

7. Ibid., 304.

8. Raúl Arredondo, "La casa soñada," *Cemento* 28 (March 1929): 16–17. Illustrated by Jorge González Camarena.

9. See for example, Leonardo Noriega Stávoli, "Quiero mi casa colonial," *Edificación* 2, no. 2 (March–April 1935): 3–5. The story is about two old friends who meet casually. One wanted a colonial house and finally obtained it, but it was expressive, cold, and unpractical, and his family got sick. The other friend was persuaded by his architect that there was no need to deliberately search for a specific style: "[His] house resulted of the better beauty because all its forms express a function that can be translated in to the health, comfort and optimism of its dwellers."

10. Juan O'Gorman, "Arquitectura técnica versus arquitectura tradicionalista," *Edificación* 2, no. 3 (May–June 1935): 10–15.

11. Mauricio Gómez Mayorga, "Casa habitación," *Arquitectura México* 7 (April 1941): 54–57.

12. The magazine (1945–50) was a private enterprise of architects Lorenzo Favela, Mauricio Gómez Mayorga, and Jorge L. Medellín.

13. Jorge L. Medellín, "Caricatura," *Arquitectura y lo demás* 1 (May 1945): 10.

14. Raúl Cacho, "Caricatura," *Arquitectura y lo demás* 2 (June 1945): 14.

15. Lorenzo Favela and Jorge L. Medellín (text), Medellín and Gómez Rosas (drawings), "La arquitectura y los muertos," *Arquitectura y lo demás* 6 (October–November 1945): 50.

16. Mauricio Gómez Mayorga, "Las personas serias pensaron . . . ," *Arquitectura y lo demás* 9 (April–August 1946): 20–21, 21.

17. See Carlos Obregón Santacilia, *Cincuenta años de arquitectura mexicana 1900-1950* (Mexico City: Patria, 1952), 76–78.

18. See Juan O'Gorman's conference, in *Pláticas sobre arquitectura 1933*, ed. Alfonso Pallares (Mexico City: Universidad Autónoma de México, 1934), 13–24.

19. See Mauricio M. Campos's conference, in *Pláticas sobre arquitectura*, 57.

20. Juan O'Gorman's conference, in *Pláticas sobre arquitectura 1933*, 13–16. For an English translation, see Luis E. Carranza, "Presentation for the Sociedad de Arquitectos Mexicanos, 1933," in *Radical Functionalism: A Social Architecture for Mexico* (New York: Routledge, 2023): 192–206.

21. Ibid., 16; translation in Carranza, "Presentation for the Sociedad de Arquitectos Mexicanos, 1933," 196.

22. Raul Castro Padilla's conference, in *Pláticas sobre arquitectura*, 48.

23. Obregón Santacilia would eventually become one of the greatest enemies of the Colonial Californiano style in his historical accounts, mainly *Cincuenta años de arquitectura mexicana*. See Jorge Pasquel's letter to Obregón Santacilia in which he describes Calles's house in Cuernavaca as Colonial Californiano in Graciela de Garay, *La obra de Carlos Obregón Santacilia, arquitecto* (Mexico City: SEP-INBA, 1979), 50.

24. With its founder Aarón Sáenz, its chair Federico T. de Lachica, and its associate Calles, FYUSA was deeply embedded in the politics of the country. See Carlos Alejandro Lupercio, *Arquitectura(s) Posrevolucionaria(s) del noreste de México* (Monterrey, Mexico: CDyAH-UANL, 2015).

25. Catherine Ettinger, *La Quinta Eréndira de Lázaro Cárdenas: de casa campestre a sede del CREFAL* (Pátzcuaro, Mexico: CREFAL; Morelia, Mexico: Universidad Michoacana de San Nicolás de Hidalgo, 2021).

26. Ibid., 23.

27. Since 1930, Aburto had designed houses for peasants in Ignacio López Bacalari's Ciudad Agrícola project; later in 1934–35, he published several articles on the matter in *Edificación*. Regarding the work with Obregón, see de Garay, *La obra de Carlos Obregón Santacilia*, 86–87.

28. Diego Rivera, "The New Mexican Architecture: A House of Carlos Obregón = La nueva arquitectura mexicana: una casa de Carlos Obregón," *Mexican Folkways* 2, no. 6 (October–November 1926): 19–29, 22.

29. See Cristina López Uribe, "Mirror Gazes: Architecture in California and México, 1915–1940," in *Found in Translation: Design in California and Mexico 1915–1985*, ed. Wendy Kaplan (Los Angeles: Los Angeles County Museum of Art, 2017), 106–11.

30. Francisco J. Serrano used marble grains to give different textures to the exterior walls. See "Entrevista con el ingeniero civil y arquitecto Francisco J. Serrano," *Construcción Mexicana* 265 (October 1981): 38–39, quoted in Lourdes Cruz González Franco, "Francisco J. Serrano. Ingeniero civil y arquitecto" (master's thesis, Universidad Autónoma de México, 1994), 52.

31. Eduardo Tejeira Davis, "Raíces novohispánicas de la arquitectura de los Estados Unidos a principios del siglo XX," *Jahrbuch für Geschichte Lateinamerikas* 20, no. 1 (December 1983): 479. Even though Eduardo Tejeira Davis is studying US architects, many of these arguments can be used in the Mexican context.

32. Manuel Toussaint, *Tasco. Su historia, sus monumentos, características actuales y posibilidades turísticas* (Mexico City: Cvltura, 1931), with drawings by Spratling, Fernández, and O'Gorman.

33. Manuel Toussaint, "Ruinas del templo franciscano de Tecali," *Arquitectura México* 8 (July 1941): 23–27, 24.

34. Juan O'Gorman, "Dos de sus obras," *Arquitectura y decoración* 3 (October 1937): 62–64.

35. Jesús T. Avecedo, *Disertaciones de un arquitecto* (Mexico City: México Moderno, 1920).

36. Oscar Wilde quoted indirectly in Ibid., 47. Page numbers are from the 1967 edition published by Ediciones de Bellas Artes. Acevedo identifies Wilde, without naming him, as "el noble forzado de la cárcel de Reading" (the forced nobleman from Reading prison). The original Oscar Wilde quote comes from "De Profundis," in *Complete Works of Oscar Wilde* (Glasgow: Harper Collins, 2003), 1032–33. Originally published in 1905.

37. Ibid., 50–51.

38. Ibid., 51.

39. Ibid., 90–91.

40. Ibid., 94–95.

41. Federico Mariscal, *La patria y la arquitectura nacional* (Mexico City: Imprenta Stephan y Torres, 1915), 10.

42. Dr. Atl, "El pabellón de México en la Exposicion de Río de Janeiro," *Azulejos* 2 (February 1922): 17.

43. Alfonso Pallares, "Índole y enseñanza de la arquitectura," *Anuario Sociedad de Arquitectos Mexicanos 1922-1923* (Mexico: Sociedad de Arquitectos Mexicanos): 86–98, 87, 89.

44. Dr. Atl, "El pabellón de México en la Exposicion de Río de Janeiro," 19.

45. Sylvester Baxter, *Spanish-Colonial Architecture in Mexico* (Boston: Millet, 1901).

46. See Cristina López Uribe, "Reflections of the 'Colonial': Between Mexico and *Californiano*," in *Latin American Modern Architectures: Ambiguous Territories*, edited by Patricio del Real and Hellen Gyger (New York: Routledge, 2013), 215–34.

47. See "Entrevista con el ingeniero civil y arquitecto Francisco J. Serrano", *Construcción Mexicana* 265 (October, 1981). Quoted in Lourdes Cruz González Franco, *Francisco J. Serrano. Ingeniero civil y arquitecto* (master's thesis, Universidad Autónoma de México, 1994), 124.

48. Aracy Amaral talked about the artificiality in São Paulo of the "Mexican style" of the 1940s. "This style incorporated into the residence the cylindrical or quadrangular tower–a false element that had no relation to the colonial construction past in Brazil, the tile panels, the wooden balconies in the Hispanic style, the needles and wrought iron ornaments. Elements also inspired by US magazines." Aracy Amaral, "La invención de un pasado," *Arquitectura neocolonial: América latina, Caribe, Estados Unidos* (São Paulo: Fondo de Cultura Económica, Fundação Memorial da América Latina, 1994),14.

49. For example, there was a diplomatic scandal when in 1930 the US ambassador Dwight Morrow commissioned Rivera to paint a mural in Cuernavaca, and he painted a critique of the Spanish Conquest. See, Ricardo Pérez Montfort, "Las peripecias diplomáticas de un mural o Diego Rivera y la hispanofobia," in *Imágenes e imaginarios sobre España en México: siglos XIX y XX* (Mexico City: Porrúa, 2007), 465–90.

HORACIO RAMOS

Adobe Modernism: Enrique Camino Brent and Colonial Architecture in Modern Peru

Is colonial-inspired architecture always a reflection of colonialist ideology? Not necessarily—and the evolution of neocolonial architecture in Lima illustrates this tension. Here, Neocolonial style refers to a group of twentieth-century buildings, projects, and theories inspired by constructions made in the Americas during the Spanish colonization.[1] Some neocolonial buildings, to be sure, catered to the middle and upper classes, evoking nostalgia for colonial society and politics. Yet others, like the house examined in this essay, emerged from an artistic vision aimed at challenging conventional norms and tastes in modern Peru.

Consider, therefore, the development of the style in Lima. The Fari house in Chosica, an upper-class suburb neighboring Lima, with its pointed arches evoking colonial buildings, was one of the style's foundational moments—a watercolor of it illustrating the September 1912 cover of the elite magazine *Ilustración Peruana* (fig. 1). Lima's main square with its neocolonial buildings, designed in 1924 but developed between 1939 and 1952 to replace the colonial-era adobe arches, was the style's most visible example.[2] The resulting buildings evoked colonial forms but were made of cement and were larger in height to accommodate present-day demographic and urban needs. These two neocolonial projects, finished four decades apart, attest to the style's prominence for much of the century.

Yet critics of the style readily noted the disconnect between neocolonial ornament and modern architectural concerns. A 1949 caricature

Fig. 1. Teófilo Castillo, *To the Marquina Family*, 1912. Reproduced on the cover of *Ilustración Peruana* (September 25, 1912). Biblioteca Nacional del Perú, Lima.

by architect Adolfo Córdova (1924–2022), published in Peru's most prestigious newspaper, *El Comercio*, crystallized this perspective (fig. 2). The drawing shows a modern-day Romeo trying to enter a window to visit his Juliette, only to hit a nonfunctional, decorative window—the same one that decorates one of the buildings on the main square. Córdova and other architects of his generation decried neocolonial architecture for nostalgically evoking the past while being at odds with notions of simplicity and functionalism spearheaded by the Swiss architect Le Corbusier (1887–1965) and the Bauhaus from the 1920s onward. As I have argued elsewhere, architects and intellectuals of Córdova's generation publicly decried neocolonial architecture through writings, talks, and caricatures in the 1940s to assert the symbolic capital of the architectural trend they valued the most—Functionalism.[3] By underscoring how the Neocolonial opposed Functionalism, these critical accounts influenced the more recent studies of architects like José García Bryce, Luis Rodríguez Cobo, or Pedro Belaunde, who have colored neocolonial architecture as anachronistic and even ideologically reactionary for its time.[4]

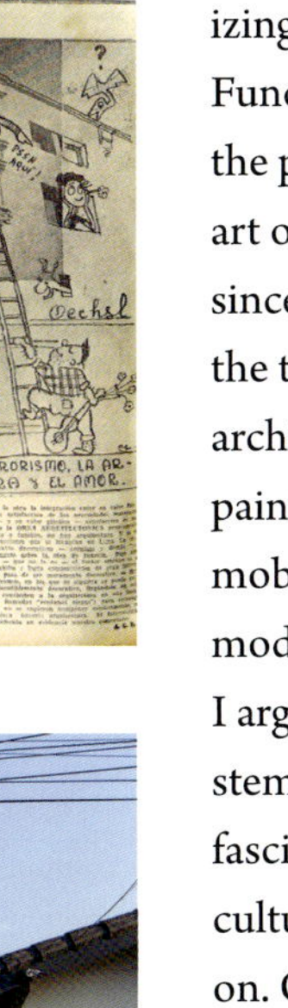
COLABORA LA AGRUPACION . ESPACIO

OLEOS DEL PINTOR PALMEIRO

CONCURSO ARQUITECTONICO

EL JARTERRORISMO, LA ARQUITECTURA Y EL AMOR

Right: Fig. 2. Adolfo Córdova, *Harth-terrorism, Architecture, and Love*, December 15, 1949. Reproduced in *El Comercio*, December 14, 1949 (afternoon edition), 8. Courtesy of the artist.

Below: Fig. 3. Enrique Camino Brent, Camino Brent Studio, San Isidro, Lima, 1943. Estate of Rafael Lemor. Photograph by Juan Pablo Murrugarra. Courtesy of the artist.

In this essay, I move away from conceptualizing neocolonial architecture in opposition to Functionalism or other architectural styles of the period (like Neoperuvian, a mix of ancient art of the Americas and colonial repertoires) since other scholars have already surveyed the tensions and intersections between these architectural trends.[5] I focus instead on how painter Enrique Camino Brent (1909–1960) mobilized colonial-era architectural imagery for modernist projects in the 1940s. In this essay, I argue that his interest in colonial architecture stemmed from Peruvian painters' increasing fascination with nonacademic art and rural culture—a context I will delve into further later on. Camino Brent's neocolonial studio, finished in 1943, materialized urban painters' interest in learning from the nonacademic aspects of rural architecture. Centering the studio—his most personal architectural project—adds nuance to our understanding of the twentieth-century appropriation of colonial art.

A Rural Facade

Camino Brent's studio is in San Isidro, an upper-class district in Lima (fig. 3). Its facade evokes the muddy adobe walls of colonial-era churches in the rural Andes—buildings that, as described below, architects had started studying systematically in the 1940s and that illustrated specialized magazine covers at the time (fig. 4). Yet the studio was made of cement.[6] Once the builders finished the bricklaying and covered it with a thick layer of cement, a *yesero* (someone specialized in working with plaster, or *yeso* in Spanish) finished the walls with several layers of plaster, producing the unfinished effect that has distinguished the facade since its 1943 completion (fig. 5). The yesero's dense treatment of specific sections, like the main window's moldings, accentuated the facade's volume (fig. 6). Furthermore, the main window is flanked by two bricks decorated with small plaster anthropomorphic figures that explicitly cite baroque ornament (fig. 7). By strategically combining plaster and cement, the building showcases multiple references to colonial rural architecture for upper-class urban audiences.

The appropriation of colonial-era models was common in Lima during the first half of the century. Rafael Marquina y Bueno (1884–1964) spearheaded colonial revival residential architecture in 1912 with his Fari house. In subsequent years, architect Emilio Harth-Terré (1899–1983) developed ambitious neocolonial projects with significant private and public economic support, including a tourist hotel in Cusco in the 1930s and the new main square buildings erected in the 1940s.[7] Since early in the 1920s, writers like Juan de Zavaleta noted the prominence of neocolonial buildings in Lima's upper- and middle-class urban landscape—a trend that continued for years.[8] Parallel to this architectural output, in the 1940s, architects like Harth-Terré and Héctor Velarde Bergmann (1898–1989) published foundational studies on colonial rural architecture.[9] While in dialogue with this architectural milieu, I argue, Camino Brent's interest in colonial forms mainly stemmed from his links to *indigenista* aesthetic frameworks.

Fig. 4. Architect Alva [sic], Church in Puno, 1944. Reproduced on the cover of *El Arquitecto Peruano* (March 1944). Museo de Arte de Lima, Biblioteca "Manuel Solari Swayne."

Fig. 5. Enrique Camino Brent, Camino Brent Studio, San Isidro, Lima, 1943. Estate of Rafael Lemor. Photograph by Juan Pablo Murrugarra. Courtesy of the artist.

Camino Brent was born in Lima in 1909 to a middle-class family of Peruvian and US backgrounds.[10] He took classes at the Escuela Nacional de Bellas Artes (National Fine Arts School) in 1922; then, in 1930, he started studying at the Escuela de Ingenieros de Lima (Lima's School of Engineers). Parallel to his architectural training, he continued his studies at Bellas Artes and graduated in 1932. José Sabogal (1888–1956)—the most influential painter of the first half of the century in Lima—was his mentor at Bellas Artes. Sabogal and Camino Brent started a lifelong friendship during this period.

Sabogal was a definitive voice in defining the interplay between nationalism, vernacular art forms, and cultural *indigenismo*.[11] Since the 1920s, indigenistas in Lima—the coastal capital, where economic and cultural elites lived—glorified the Indigenous peoples in the rural Andes as a source of cultural particularity for the nation.[12] Sabogal considered that the country needed to foreground its mestizo cultural identity; in order for it to be a contender in the international sphere, it needed Native particularity but also to be modern. It could not be exclusively Indigenous, a concept he linked to a static, dying past.[13]

Fig. 6. Enrique Camino Brent, Camino Brent Studio, San Isidro, Lima, 1943. Estate of Rafael Lemor. Photograph by Juan Pablo Murrugarra. Courtesy of the artist.

Sabogal sought the material evidence of *mestizaje* in colonial-era rural architecture and present-day handmade crafts from the southern Andes. In 1928, he celebrated the theories of Argentine architects like Martín Noel (1888–1963) and Ángel Guido (1896–1960), who argued that Andean colonial architecture crystallized the interplay of the Spanish baroque with an Indigenous "spirit."[14] And in 1929, he argued that carved gourds from Huancayo (a small city in southern Peru) married "Spanish realism" with "aboriginal decorative rhythm."[15] Through publications and talks, indigenistas like Sabogal posited colonial architecture and present-day crafts as the materialization of the blurry, never fully defined concept of mestizaje.[16]

Modernists' glorification of *arte popular* also asserted a conceptual distance between them and rural artists, as noted by scholars like Mirko Lauer and Natalia Majluf.[17] While *artistas populares* were the carriers of the nation's traditional aesthetics, artists like Sabogal were the only ones modern enough to renew them. This cultural hierarchy was racialized and naturalized against the Quechua-speaking artists living in rural areas. This becomes clear when one considers, as Gabriela Germana Roquez has highlighted, that while indigenistas celebrated rural arts, they rarely embraced such media in their own oeuvres.[18] They continued using painting, sculpture, and woodcut—media associated with fine and modernist arts. Camino Brent was the exception that proved the rule.

Inspired by Sabogal, Camino Brent traveled to Puno, in the southern Peruvian Andes, in 1937.[19] There, he studied figurative clay ceramic from Checca Pupuja, prompting foundational studies in the 1950s by Sabogal and himself on what became known as Pucará bulls.[20] Around these years, he also encountered and learned how to fabricate *chuas*—plates with decorative figures of animals and plants produced in Puno

Fig. 7. Enrique Camino Brent, Camino Brent Studio, San Isidro, Lima, 1943. Estate of Rafael Lemor. Photograph by Juan Pablo Murrugarra. Courtesy of the artist.

Fig. 8. Camino Brent's Studio, 1945. Reproduced in *El Arquitecto Peruano* (February 1945). Museo de Arte de Lima, Biblioteca "Manuel Solari Swayne."

Fig. 9. Camino Brent's Studio, 1945. Reproduced in *El Arquitecto Peruano* (February 1945). Museo de Arte de Lima, Biblioteca "Manuel Solari Swayne."

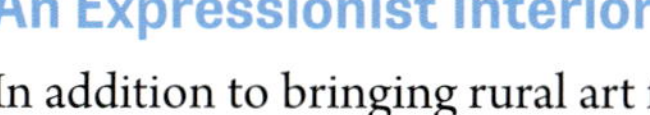

Fig. 10. Enrique Camino Brent, *La escalera roja* (The Red Stair), 1954. Oil on canvas, 23¼ × 23¼ in. (59 × 59 cm). Pinacoteca Municipal Ignacio Merino, Lima, Peru.

and Cusco, at least since the nineteenth century.[21] Later on, he taught courses on how to make them, first at the Escuela Politécnica (Technical School) in Lima in the late 1940s and then at the Escuela de Bellas Artes (Fine Arts School) in Huamanga, Ayacucho. These pedagogical projects evidence a personal commitment to revitalizing rural arts beyond their rhetorical glorification. To produce and disseminate rural ceramic techniques was a statement about their modernity.

Camino Brent's 1943 studio made a similar statement. The artist drew inspiration from the bell towers of colonial-era churches but divorced them from their original religious context. By secularizing them, the dense and rough texture of the walls evoked the aesthetic dimension of Andean rural materials. To be sure, architects like Harth-Terré also analyzed these vernacular elements in their monographs of the 1940s. But Camino Brent put them on display in one of Lima's most exclusive districts at a time when—as social scientists like José Matos have noted—Lima's reactionary elites looked down on the increasing number of migrants coming to the capital from Andean cities and towns.[22] Within that specific framework, Camino Brent's studio affirmed the modernity of Andean rural culture.

An Expressionist Interior

In addition to bringing rural art forms to an upper-class residential architecture in Lima, Camino Brent used them for the avant-garde space par excellence—the artist studio. As noted by art historian Jorge Rivas, artists' studios were "testing grounds" for modernist experimentation.[23] That was, to be sure, the case of Juan O'Gorman's house studio for Frida Kahlo (1907–1954) and Diego Rivera (1886–1957), built between 1929 and 1931 in Mexico City.[24] Echoing the ideas and designs of Le Corbusier, O'Gorman's project for these renowned Mexican painters posited geometric volumes and open floorplans for modern living and working. But while O'Gorman's house studio was groundbreaking for the functionalist design of its studio spaces, Camino Brent's modernism was groundbreaking, I contend here, in its impracticality.

The facade's balconies are inspired by colonial houses' balconies, which Camino Brent painted in southern Andean cities like Puno and Ayacucho in the 1930s. To support them, he designed large cement moldings covered by successive layers of lime and plaster. This thick, unfinished layering gave the overall facade a sense of weight, thus contrasting with the Rivera-Kahlo studio's comparatively more straightforward, cleaner facades. The interior environment of Camino Brent's studio also asserted an impractical sense of weight. The studio comprises a relatively small room with an easel and a worktable and a larger room with a window connecting to the patio (fig. 8). These two spaces are separated by a large arch crowned by a wooden balcony. To the arch's left, a large staircase interrupts a substantial part of the studio's smaller room (fig. 9). As the artist's son, Federico Camino, has noted, the rooms' disconcerting design often prompted a sense of claustrophobia in visitors: a sensibility of unease and partial discomfort.

In that regard, the studio's intricate design evokes the expressionist aesthetics of his paintings. Consider Camino Brent's 1954 painting *La escalera roja* (The Red Staircase) depicting the interior of a monastery in Cusco (fig. 10). The painter applied deep impasto to depict the monastery's white walls, evoking rural architecture's unfinished layers of plaster and mud. On the right side, a white arch frames the overall composition; to its left, the vertical wooden columns that support the tile roof take on an uncannily curved shape, echoing the arch and walls. At the center, two women wearing black robes walk down the large staircase that connects the building's four stories. Camino Brent's rendering of the stairs, which switches direction from left to right and back on each floor, partially disorients the spectator. This disconcerting effect is further exacerbated by the bright red pigment of the staircase's top section, which breaks with the canvas' muted tones and directs the viewer's curiosity to a scene beyond the picture frame.

The unease prompted by Camino Brent's studio and painting stands out when compared to the experience of seeing his mentor's sole architecture project. In 1929, Sabogal designed what he called a "Yunka Style" home or "Ornamental Huaca" (Sacred Site; fig. 11).[25] Its lower section resembles the mud-made, no-longer colored walls of Chan Chan Temple, built around 850 CE by the Chimú, an Indigenous culture from northern Peru. The upper level, in its turn, consists of a bright yellow building with a red rooftop and geometric patterns echoing Chimú designs.[26] Sabogal's project was located at the recently finished Parque de la Reserva (Reserve Park) in the middle-class district of Santa Beatríz. The eight-hectare park was one of the last large-scale urban projects sponsored by President Augusto

Fig. 11. José Sabogal, Ornamental Huaca in the Reserve Park, Lima, Peru, 1929. Photograph by Pablo Cruz. Courtesy of the artist.

B. Leguía's administration (1919–30).[27] Thus, the Ornamental Huaca posited a celebratory take on Indigenous art in dialogue with Leguía's populist celebration of those communities. Its lower wall, however, actually distanced the building from visitors, who saw in it an ornament to contemplate from a distance. While Sabogal's project constituted a monumental ornament to look at from afar, Camino Brent's studio deployed ornament to bolster an embodied experience in the visitor.

Below: Fig. 12. Humberto Guerra, House in Chosica, 1945. Reproduced in *El Arquitecto Peruano* (March 1945). Museo de Arte de Lima, Biblioteca "Manuel Solari Swayne."

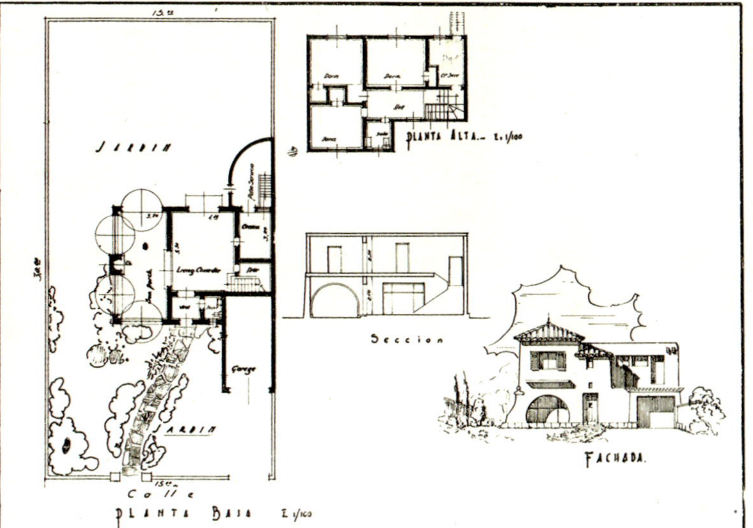

Camino Brent developed his studio in 1943, when President Leguía's sponsorship of neocolonial and neoperuvian architecture was a somewhat distant echo. Aside from the buildings in the main square (designed in 1924 but only executed from 1939 to 1952), neocolonial architecture became increasingly uncommon in public-sponsored projects. The style returned to the suburban contexts where the Fari house had kickstarted the movement in 1912. In 1945, architect Humberto Guerra designed a large house outside Lima in the upper-class suburb of Chosica (fig. 12).[28] The house's clean, geometric facade and large, open-floorplan interiors with ample windows spoke to current modernist trends, while its arch-like main window and tile roof evoked historical references.

Camino Brent developed his most ambitious neocolonial project in the 1950s—the various buildings and open-air galleries that comprised the Montesierpe hacienda in Humay, a rural district in the Pisco province, south of Lima.[29] But like similar contemporary projects, Guerra's house and the Montesierpe hacienda crystalized a new direction—neocolonial architecture receded from the capital, only to find a place in the suburbs.

As noted above, functionalist architects like Adolfo Córdova published scathing critiques against the modern appropriation of colonial forms. Architect Luis Miró Quesada Garland (1914–1994), writing for Agrupación Espacio, a group he belonged to alongside Córdova, argued that indigenista painting and neocolonial architecture followed "empty myths."[30] Embracing abstract painting and functionalist architecture, by contrast, would bring the artistic milieu "up to date." As colonial architecture became a topic of historical research for architects like Harth-Terré and Velarde, it ceased to inspire modern architecture. Echoing Sabogal's and Camino Brent's trips to the southern Andes of the

1930s, young architecture students like Roberto Wakeham (1920–1986) visited rural churches and studied them as part of their training at the Escuela de Ingenieros, but after graduating, they developed functionalist buildings.[31]

Camino Brent's studio's relatively simple and geometric facade did dialogue with Functionalism. However, its handmade, unfinished-looking moldings and its interior spaces asserted Camino Brent's specific vision. As noted by architect Elio Martuccelli, the yesero profession disappeared in the 1940s and 1950s, when functionalist architects and engineers privileged clean facades.[32] Unlike functionalist architects of the period, Camino Brent posited that geometric, simple forms could welcome multilayered ornament. Modern architecture could include colonial forms.

Conclusion

In modern Mexico, as noted by Cristina López Uribe, architects like Luis Barragán (1902–1988) married vernacular references with functionalist aesthetics in the 1950s and 1960s.[33] Later, in the 1980s, British architect Kenneth Frampton (born 1930) coined the term Critical Regionalism to describe the "reaction to global modernization" that developed in countries as varied as Mexico, Japan, Denmark, and Brazil, and which foregrounded autochthonous cultures and materials.[34] In Peru, the intersection of modernist and vernacular forms did not crystallize into a broader trend as in other countries. Camino Brent's architectural projects of the 1940s and 1950s, thus, stood out as a rarity.

One of the first instances of what could be labeled as Critical Regionalism, as discussed

Fig. 13. Juvenal Baracco, Casa Ghezzi, Lima, Peru. Designed in 1983 and constructed in 1984. Photograph courtesy of Juvenal Baracco.

by art historian Dorota Biczel, was the Ghezzi beach house outside of Lima, designed in 1983 by Limeño architect Juvenal Baracco (born 1940; fig. 13).[35] The house included areas covered by bamboo-cane rooftops and walls that welcomed light and ventilation into common areas. Baracco's project responded to reductive understandings of Le Corbusier's ideas, which restricted the uses of vernacular materials like bamboo.[36] Similarly, a few years earlier, in 1979, architect Augusto Ortíz de Zevallos (born 1949) wrote an insightful critique of local functionalism that vindicated the aesthetic contributions of "Peruvianist historicisms," like the Neocolonial and Neoperuavianism, in the first half of the twentieth century.[37]

Only in the 1980s did architects like Baracco or Ortíz de Zevallos challenge reductive understandings of Functionalism through buildings and writings that foregrounded rural culture and historical references. But decades before postmodern architects and "critical regionalists," Camino Brent had already argued that rural materials and methods offered an illuminating entryway into modernity. At his studio, he looked into colonial history to imagine alternative ways to be modern.

Notes

1. Peruvian architect Héctor Velarde wrote one of the earliest historical accounts of the style's development in Lima. See Héctor Velarde, *Obras completas IV: ensayos, artículos estéticos* (Lima, Peru: Francisco Moncloa Editores, 1966), 309–17.

2. On the main square buildings, see Teresa Abad and Samuel Cárdenas, "Evolución histórica del espacio urbano de la Plaza Mayor de Lima" (bachelor's thesis, Universidad Nacional de Ingeniería, 1975). For a study focused on the 1940s reform, see Horacio Ramos, "Destrucción y reinvención de la plaza de Armas. Estilo neocolonial y modernización urbana en Lima, 1924-1954" (master's thesis, Pontificia Universidad Católica del Perú, 2014).

3. Horacio Ramos, "La reforma neocolonial de la plaza de Armas. Modernización urbana y patrimonio arquitectónico en Lima, 1901-1952," *Histórica* 40, no. 1 (2016): 102–42.

4. José García Bryce, "Arquitectura peruana," *Boletín. Sociedad de Arquitectos del Perú* 7 (April–June 1959): 38–40; Luis Rodríguez Cobos, *Arquitectura limeña: paisajes de una utopía* (Lima: Fondo Editorial Colegio de Arquitectos del Perú, 1983), 35–46; Pedro Belaúnde, "Perú: mito, esperanza y realidad en la búsqueda de raíces nacionales," in *Arquitectura neocolonial. América Latina, el Caribe, Estados Unidos*, ed. Aracy A. Amaral (São Paulo: Fundación Memorial de América Latina, Fondo de Cultura Económica, 1994), 74–94. For a discussion of the literature on neocolonial architecture, see "Introducción" in Ramos, "Destrucción y reinvención de la Plaza de Armas."

5. See Luis Eduardo Wuffarden, "Manuel Piqueras Cotolí, neoperuano de ambos mundos," in *Manuel Piqueras Cotolí: arquitecto, escultor y urbanista entre España y el Perú*, ed. Luis Eduardo Wuffarden (Lima, Peru: Museo de Arte de Lima, 2003), 21–61; Gabriel Ramón, *El Neoperuano: arqueología, estilo nacional y paisaje urbano en Lima, 1910-1940* (Lima, Peru: Municipalidad Metropolitana de Lima, Sequilao Editores, 2014); Wiley Ludeña Urquizo, *Tres buenos tigres: Piqueras – Belaunde – La Agrupación Espacio:vanguardia y urbanismo en el Perú del siglo XX* (Lima: Colegio de Arquitectos del Perú, Regional Junín, 2004); Elio Martuccelli, *Arquitectura para una ciudad fragmentada: ideas, proyectos y edificios en la Lima del siglo XX*, 2nd ed. (Lima, Peru: Universidad Ricardo Palma, 2017), 69–257. In this volume, Cristina López Uribe's essay analyzes the tensions and intersections between Functionalism and neocolonial architecture in Mexico.

6. Federico Camino, in conversation with the author, August 8, 2022. I sincerely thank Federico Camino for sharing his insights and perspective on his father's oeuvre (through multiple phone calls and email exchanges), which shaped some of this article's arguments.

7. For a survey of Harth-Terré's work, see Gladys Pinillos and Noris Pinillos, "Harth-terré, arquitecto" (bachelor's thesis, Universidad Nacional de Ingeniería, 1982). For an analysis of the main square reform, see Ramos, "La reforma neocolonial de la plaza de Armas."

8. Juan de Zavaleta, "El renacimiento de la arquitectura colonial en Lima," *Mundial*, no. 103 (May 5, 1922): [6–7].

9. See Emilio Harth-Terré, "Arquitectura virreinal y arquitectura moderna," *El Arquitecto Peruano*, no. 42 (January 1941): [29–30]. He systematized his studies in the 1960s. See Emilio Harth-Terré, "La arquitectura mestiza del sur peruano," *Revista Histórica* 27 (1965): 285–93. See also Velarde, *Obras ompletas IV*.

10. The biographical information I use here stems from Eduardo Moll's comprehensive monograph on Camino Brent and my interview with the artist's son. See Eduardo Moll, ed., *Enrique Camino Brent, 1909-1960* (Lima, Peru: Editorial Navarrete, 1988).

11. Sabogal considered that the country's "authentic" culture was localized in the southern Andes and was at odds with Lima's aristocratic culture. José Sabogal was born in a low-income household in Cajabamba, Cajamarca, in Peru's northern Andes. But Sabogal spent most of his career in Lima. See Natalia Majluf and Luis Eduardo Wuffarden, "José Sabogal, 'primer pintor peruano,'" in *Sabogal*, eds. Natalia Majluf and Luis Eduardo Wuffarden (Lima, Peru: Museo de Arte de Lima, 2013), 2–124.

12. *Indigenismo* refers to a broad grouping of discourses in politics, the social sciences, and the arts concerned with ennobling Indigenous peoples in Latin American nations. With its heyday between the 1920s and 1940s, indigenismo was often linked to nationalist politics and

discourses voiced by non-Indigenous members of the cultural elite. See Majluf and Wuffarden, "José Sabogal."

13. For Sabogal's ideas of cultural mestizaje, see Fernando Villegas Torres, *José Sabogal y la escuela peruana mestiza: el Instituto de Arte Peruano (1931-1973)* (Lima, Peru: Universidad Nacional Mayor de San Marcos, fonda Editorial, 2020), 19–51, 83–99.

14. Don Quijote [Carlos Solari], "Notas de arte. Entrevista con José Sabogal," *Mundial* 8, no. 439 (November 9, 1928): 54–55.

15. J. A. S. [José Sabogal], "Los 'mates' y el yaraví," *Amauta*, no. 26 (September-October 1929): 18.

16. See Ananda Cohen-Aponte, "Forging a Popular Art History: *Indigenismo* and the Art of Colonial Peru," *RES: Anthropology and Aesthetics*, nos. 67–68 (2016/2017): 273–89.

17. See Mirko Lauer, *Crítica de la artesanía: plástica y sociedad en los Andes peruanos* (Lima, Peru: Centro de Estudios y Promoción del Desarrollo, 1982); Natalia Majluf, "El indigenismo en México y Perú: hacia una mirada comparativa," in *Arte, historia e identidad en América: visiones comparativas*, vol. 2, ed. Gustavo Curiel, Renato González Mello, and Juana Gutiérrez Haces (Mexico City: Universidad Nacional Autónoma de México, 1994), 611–28.

18. Gabriela Germana Roquez, "The Tablas de Sarhua: Indigenous Aesthetics in the Context of Contemporary Peruvian Art" (PhD dissertation, The Florida State University, 2021), 183. See also Giuliana Borea, "Arte popular y la imposibilidad de sujetos contemporáneos; o la estructura del pensamiento moderno y la racialización del arte," in *Arte y antropología: estudios, encuentros y nuevos horizontes*, ed. Giuliana Borea (Lima: Pontificia Universidad Católica del Perú, 2017), 97–119.

19. For an overview of this context, see Villegas, *José Sabogal y la escuela peruana mestiza*, 29–56.

20. For an analysis of Sabogal's and Camino Brent's studies on art of this region, see Fernando Villegas, "Entre la tradición mestiza y su modernidad contemporánea: El toro de Pucará visto por José Sabogal y Enrique Camino Brent," in *Toro, torito de Pucará: galería y estudios*, ed. Jesús Ruiz Durand (Lima, Peru: Ministerio de Comercio Exterior y Turismo, MINCETUR, 2010), 32–37.

21. On *chuas*, see Sara Acevedo, "La loza de la tierra: cerámica vidriada en el Perú," in *La loza de la tierra: cerámica vidriada en el Perú*, ed. Sara Acevedo (Lima, Peru: Universidad Ricardo Palma, Instituto Cultural Peruano Norteamericano, 2004), 16–39.

22. José Matos Mar, *Desborde popular y crisis del Estado:el nuevo rostro del Perú en la década de 1980* (Lima, Peru: Instituto de Estudios Peruanos, 1984).

23. Jorge Rivas, "Cannibal Homes: Additive Modernity and Design by Absorption in Brazil, Mexico, and Venezuela, 1940–1970," in *Moderno: Design for Living in Brazil, Mexico, and Venezuela, 1940–1978*, ed. Gabriela Rangel and Jorge Rivas (New York: Americas Society, 2015), 14–33.

24. See Javier Jerez González, *O'Gorman, Kahlo, Rivera: encuentro para una arquitectura revolucionaria* (Buenos Aires: Diseño, 2021). For an insightful reading of the house, see Cristina López Uribe, "Mirror Gazes: Architecture in California and Mexico, 1915–1940," in *Found in Translation: Design in California and Mexico, 1915–1985*, ed. Wendy Caplan (Los Angeles: Los Angeles County Museum of Art, 2017), 112–14.

25. For an analysis of the Ornamental Huaca, see Ramón, *El Neoperuano*, 89–94. In Quechua, a huaca or wak'a is an object that represents something revered, typically a monument of some kind. See Encyclopædia Britannica, "Inca Religion: Temples and Shrines," accessed March 25, 2024, https://www.britannica.com/topic/Inca-religion#ref345011.

26. For an account on contemporaneous studies of Chan Chan, see Otto Holstein, "Chan-Chan: Capital of the Great Chimu," *Geographical Review* 17, no. 1 (January 1927): 36–61.

27. For a recent analysis of Leguía's administration, with a few essays that discuss the role of culture, see Paulo Drinot, ed., *La Patria Nueva: Economía, sociedad y cultura en el Perú, 1919-1930* (Raleigh: University of North Carolina Press, 2018).

28. This and other neocolonial projects were reproduced in *El Arquitecto Peruano* (March 1945).

29. Federico Camino in conversation with the author via Zoom, August 8, 2022. It goes beyond the scope of this paper to analyze this ambitious project of the 1950s, which I have not had the opportunity to see in person yet.

30. Agrupación Espacio, "Expresión de principios de la Agrupación Espacio," *El Comercio*, May 15, 1947, 3-4. For an alaysis, see Ricardo Kusunoki, "Szyszlo y la batalla por la abstracción (1947–1955)," in *Szyszlo*, eds. Luis Eduardo Wuffarden and Ricardo Kusunoki (Lima, Peru: Museo de Arte de Lima, 2011), 54–70.

31. One of Wakehman's sketches was reproduced in *El Arquitecto Peruano* (April 1944).

32. Martuccelli, *Arquitectura para una ciudad fragmentada*, 125.

33. For an analysis of Barragán's "Vernacular Modernism," see López Uribe, "Mirror Gazes," 84–115. For an overview of Barragán's oeuvre, see Louise Noelle, ed., *El legado de Luis Barragán, 1902-2002* (Mexico City: Instituto Nacional de Bellas Artes, 2002).

34. Kenneth Frampton, "Regionalismo crítico: arquitectura moderna e identidad cultural," *Proa* 354 (September 1986): 20–23. For a critical reading of the concept of Critical Regionalism, see Keith L. Eggener, "Placing Resistance: A Critique of Critical Regionalism," *Journal of Architectural Education* 55, no. 4 (May 2002): 228–37.

35. Dorota Biczel, "Viewpoint: Self-Construction, Vernacular Materials, and Democracy Building: Los Bestias, Lima, 1984–1987," *Buildings & Landscapes: Journal of the Vernacular Architecture Forum* 20, no. 2 (2013): 1–21.

36. On Baracco's work, see Juvenal Baracco, *Juvenal Baracco: un universe en casa* (Bogota, Colombia: Universidad de los Andes, 1988). For an analysis of this period, see Martucelli, *Arquitectura para una ciudad fragmentada*, 266–80.

37. Augusto Ortíz de Zevallos, "Las ideas versus las imágenes: cuestiones al debate arquitectónico peruano," *Apuntes. Revista de ciencias sociales* 9 (1979): 87–110.

RICARDO KUSUNOKI RODRÍGUEZ

Aesthetics of Excess: Lima's Neocolonial Imaginary (1870–1950)

ore than true admiration, the success of a neocolonial imaginary in Lima revealed an ambivalent attitude toward actual viceregal art and architecture. For if revaluing colonial culture and finding inspiration in it to create a true national art was the challenge that gave meaning to the neocolonial horizon in Lima, this attitude was always tinged with contradiction. In the midst of the Hispanist furor of the 1920s and 1930s, nationalism would not cease to sustain its rhetoric on the promise of material progress for the Peruvian capital, whose old quarters continued to serve as the nation's administrative center. Progress itself seemed to have a special physical consistency—that of cement—which had little to do with adobe, wood, reeds, or plaster, omnipresent elements in the city's old buildings. Even local pride in the best examples of colonial architecture surviving in Lima seemed to demand the opening of large plazas or avenues with the explicit purpose of enhancing those constructions. Although carrying out such urban projects would mean demolishing entire blocks of the old city, it also opened up the possibility for the capital to take on the monumentality of large modern cities, erecting imposing neocolonial-style structures where humble colonial constructions rarely exceeding two stories had previously stood.

In fact, the nationalist perspective did not establish sharp distinctions between historical truth and fiction. In the discourses that gave meaning to the nation, the great colonial constructions that still existed came to be combined with a modern mass culture, as if both were of equal standing, so that anecdote could replace great historical narratives. Visual creators and modern spectators also interpreted legendary colonial riches in a modern way: as an accumulation of goods approximating the bourgeois ideal of consumption. Thus, far from any desire for accuracy, the viceroyalty became a projection in the past of that material progress which looked to the future. From that perspective, the most representative element of the colonial heritage would be an exceptional building such as the famous Torre Tagle Palace, which was anything but typical of Lima architecture. But it was more problematic to deal with the universe of viceregal objects, especially because the anecdotal vision of the past that made the colonial period attractive had almost no direct relation to the paintings, sculptures, or decorative arts of that period that survived in the present. Hence, the project of recovering the spirit of colonial times would have to overcome the limitations of the actual material culture of the viceregal period, to the point of blurring the boundaries between originals, recreations, and forgeries. A gap emerged between the material heritage of that past and the modern aspirations of nationalism that the Neocolonial style, in all its modernity, was called upon to fill.

The Equivocal Riches of the Viceroyalty

Already in 1907, even before the consolidation of a true nationalist horizon among the local intelligentsia, the young intellectual José de la Riva Agüero y Osma rehearsed one of the first modern arguments for the preservation of Lima's viceregal architecture.[1] Riva Agüero directed his comments against the many remodeling projects that recently had been undertaken on several colonial churches in the Peruvian capital. But his attention was focused, above all, on the most ambitious of those works: the reconstruction of the church of San Agustín. Over a decade earlier, in 1895, the temple's great tower had been one of the main sites where the clash between the troops of political leader Nicolás de Piérola and those of President Andrés Avelino Cáceres was fought (fig. 1). The damages that the building suffered, however, were nothing more than a pretext to undertake its total modernization, with a radicality that had no local precedents. In fact, the Augustinian friars opted to demolish a good part of the structure to erect another of "Romanesque" appearance that, in their opinion, would blend in well with those sections of the Spanish colonial style preserved from the old church, especially the impressive stone facade built at the beginning of the eighteenth century (fig. 2).[2] For Riva Agüero, this could only be considered a flagrant adulteration of one of

Right: Fig. 1. Church of San Agustín de Lima after the revolution of 1895. In *Souvenir of the inauguration of the temple of San Agustín*(Lima, Peru: Imprenta de E. Moreno, 1908). Collection of Luis Eduardo Wuffarden, Lima, Peru.

Far right: Fig. 2. José Carreras's project for the remodel of the Church of San Agustín de Lima. In *Souvenir of the inauguration of the temple of San Agustín* (Lima, Peru: Imprenta de E. Moreno, 1908), 45. Collection of Luis Eduardo Wuffarden, Lima, Peru.

the most important testimonies of the city's colonial past. But his defense of that architectural monument did not imply an aesthetic embrace of its "frizzy churrigueresque style," which the author considered a decadent artistic expression. In fact, the young writer affirmed quite explicitly that, certainly, San Agustín—as, for that matter, the other viceregal temples of Lima—was not "a work of art nor deserves the consideration as such."[3] In his opinion, those buildings should be preserved for their capacity to evoke the history of the country even if they lacked true aesthetic merit, since, in his own words, "there is no architectural decadence that, seen through the centuries, lacks poetic suggestion."[4]

Riva Agüero's peculiar appraisal of colonial monuments was consistent with his intellectual interests, focused on building a sense of national belonging based on a critical and affective view of the past. The viceregal Lima that he considered a decadent "Byzantium" was also home to an aristocracy from which he proudly descended. His appraisal of a large part of the viceroyalty's intellectual production had been equally negative when he published *Carácter de la literatura del Perú Independiente* (Character of the literature of independent Peru), a brilliant text with which he obtained his bachelor of arts degree in 1905.[5] But the same attitude led him to defend, in the book's conclusions, fidelity to the purity of the Spanish language and literary canon, especially in the face of the onslaught of French modernist influence.[6] It is thus not surprising that his main reference for a national literature should have been *Tradiciones peruanas* (Peruvian Traditions), short, historically evocative stories written by the Lima-born Ricardo Palma between the last third of the nineteenth century and the beginning of the twentieth century. Riva Agüero recognized that Palma's talent reached its maximum expression in narratives staged in colonial times, a period that he saw disastrously projected

Fig. 3. "Pancho" Fierro, *The lady of the imperial cot*, ca. 1870–79. Watercolor on paper, 9¼ × 7⅛ in. (23.5 × 18.1 cm). Pinacoteca Municipal Ignacio Merino, Municipalidad Metropolitana de Lima.

in the country's present: it created "the habit of indolence, annulled activity and character, generated debility like a warm perfumed bath."[7] Transformed into tradition, the viceroyalty acquired evocative powers: "judging things with the criteria of an artist, and not with the criteria of a sociologist and politician, it is necessary to recognize that it has a certain charm, like that of a narcotic that gently relaxes the tissues and spreads a delicious laxity throughout the body."[8]

Riva Agüero was not exaggerating when he claimed that Palma "revived among us the feelings of our ancestors."[9] Throughout successive installments that began in 1872, Palma's *Tradiciones peruanas* had been modeling the ways

Right: Fig. 4. "Pancho" Fierro, *Tapada*, ca. 1850–60. Watercolor on paper, 10⅛ × 7⅝ in. (25.7 × 19.4 cm). Museo de Arte de Lima: Grupo de donantes 1995.

Below: Fig. 5. Attributed to Francisco Javier Cortés, *Woman in a Lima dress between 1760 and 1780*, ca. 1827–38. Watercolor and tempera on paper, 9½ × 7⅛ in. (24.1 × 18.1 cm). Museo de Arte de Lima: Donación Juan Carlos Verme.

of imagining the Peruvian past, and especially the viceregal period, for an increasingly wider reading public. But that monumental literary contribution was not initially accompanied by any significant visual counterpart. Except for portraits and a few rare commemorative images, most colonial painting dealt with religious themes and only rarely offered an explicit account of its surroundings or everyday reality. To imagine what life had been like in the viceregal period, one could rely on the broad repertoire of genre paintings created by "Pancho" Fierro (1810–1879) in the mid-nineteenth century, whose images Palma himself collected as if true documents of the past.[10] Fierro's works, however, described relatively recent types and customs that Palma himself could contrast with his own experience or with the recollections of his peers (fig. 3). The image of Lima on the eve of independence thus appeared as a city of endearing but provincial customs, whose mansions were characterized by an austere and heavy sense of elegance. The writer had even claimed that the costume of the famous *tapadas* (veiled women) acquired its most emblematic form in republican times, assuming an elegance that contrasted with the somewhat caricatured way in which late colonial *limeñas* dressed (figs. 4 and 5).[11]

When Palma was born in 1833, Lima was just beginning to recover from the turmoil in which it was plunged after the wars of independence, so it was difficult to find anything like the mythical displays of opulence narrated by colonial chroniclers. Barely a few years later, he would witness the growing abyss that emerged between the universe of objects inherited from the viceregal period and a new, fully bourgeois consumer culture, stimulated by an industrial production that flooded the country with the opening of trade. Faced with this contrast between past and present, Palma would come to see the legendary wealth of the old viceregal capital as a negation of the ideal of progress, inevitably distant from the comfort, sophistication, and abundance characterizing modern life.

As early as 1832, the liberal politician Manuel Lorenzo de Vidaurre noted the advantages of free trade, condescendingly recalling "what our furniture, our dinnerware, our clothes, our shoes were like forty years earlier, when Peru was very rich."[12] "Prevent imports to Peru," he warned against the possibility of returning to the past, "and industry will lose what we have advanced: we will again have couches, cushions, bunks, cabinets."[13] But the above process only intensified in the mid-nineteenth century, when local elites became suddenly rich thanks to guano exports. In one of his most famous *tradiciones*, dedicated to a society ball held in Lima in 1855, Palma noted how the women of the new guano bourgeoisie showed their power by wearing gold jewelry, much more expensive than the silver jewelry worn by the descendants of the old colonial nobility.[14] Progress seemed to become even more evident in 1873, the year after Palma's *Tradiciones peruanas* appeared, when Lima's elite competed to wear the most expensive attire at a ball held at the Club Nacional. As historian Paul Rizo Patrón recalls, the winner was Rosa Elguera de Laos, who disguised herself as Anne of Austria, importing exorbitant costumes and jewelry from Paris (fig. 6).[15] None of the costumes of the other participants evoked colonial times; rather, they turned to European characters, as if guano riches led to forgetting local specificity so as to assert full membership in the "civilized order" of the most powerful Western nations.

The Visual Definition of a Trope

In 1883, a decade after the famous ball at the Club Nacional, the Peruvian State faced its devastating defeat in the War of the Pacific, a four-year conflict that had left the country virtually bankrupt. In that context, not only was

Fig. 6. Estudio Courret, Rosa Elguera de Laos en disfraz de *Ana de Austria*, 1873. Photograph on albuminated paper, 6½ × 4¼ in. (16.5 × 10.8 cm). Museo de Arte de Lima: Comité de Formación de Colecciones 2019. Donación Maki Miró Quesada.

it impossible to sustain any illusion of progress, but it was also necessary to search for the failures that had triggered the crisis. However, that same year, Palma published a new expanded edition of his *Tradiciones peruanas*, as if those ironic but affectionate evocations of local history could open up a truce between the present and a past that was considered the cause of all evils.[16] This explains why admiration for Palma's work grew in parallel to a perspective that, though ever more critical of the colonial past, sought an anchor for the nation's identity in intimate stories associated with family memories and anecdotes, as opposed to grand historical narratives. As Javier Prado Ugarteche suggested, "Sad and painful is, indeed, gentlemen, the impression left on our spirit by the history of our ancestors! Justly, the nineteenth century condemns that history; but, nevertheless, in its criticism one can observe a seal of benevolence. For in the depths of that sad history, at the center of that morally and intellectually sick organism, of that weak, idle, vicious and courtesan society, we feel the beats of a noble and generous heart and we perceive the flashes of a superior intelligence."[17]

But if the viceregal Hispanic heritage could be contested, Spain itself was an actual nation connected to Peru by diverse interests, especially after the end of all hostilities with the signing of a treaty of friendship in 1879. As historian Mariela Mondragón recalls, it was no coincidence that the previous year Palma had attempted to publish his *Tradiciones peruanas* in Madrid, taking advantage of his appointment as a corresponding member of the Real Academia de la Lengua.[18] In fact, the growing ubiquity of a *castizo*, that is a pure or authentic "Hispanic" culture, in late-nineteenth-century Lima—as well as in urban culture throughout the region—was not a simple extension of colonial times.

It came from vast modern literary, graphic, and musical repertoires, whose circulation in the old colonies made it possible to forge a powerful sense of community throughout Spanish-speaking territories. Only at the end of the nineteenth century would local intellectuals end up fully vindicating the Spanish Conquest not only as the source of a common past but also as an inescapable mark of identity that counterposed the region to the capitalist pragmatism of "Anglo-Saxon culture," represented by the United States and its predominance over the region. This process would reach one of its culminating moments in 1892, when the four hundredth anniversary of the discovery of America was celebrated with the organization of the *American Historical Exposition* in Madrid, in which most of the Latin American countries participated.[19]

In this context, it is not surprising that in 1893 Palma should publish his *Tradiciones peruanas* in Barcelona.[20] Nothing was more appropriate to popularize his work than to publish in a country that the writer himself considered to be the focal point of a broader Hispanic intellectual circuit. Added to this was the importance of the

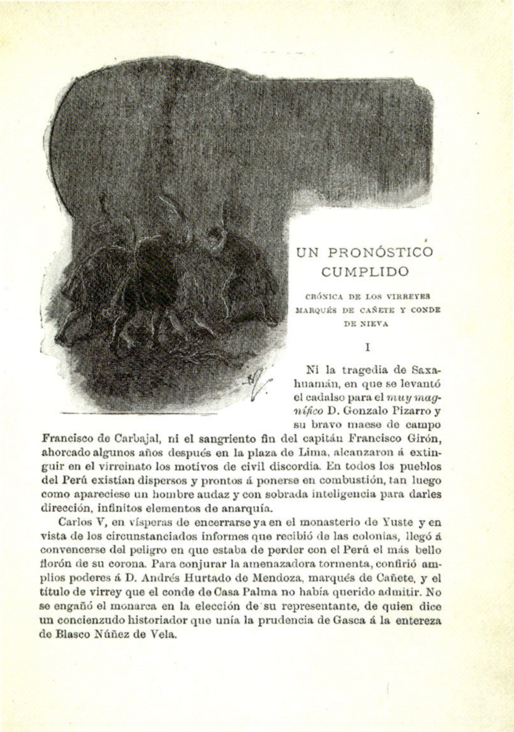

UN PRONÓSTICO CUMPLIDO

CRÓNICA DE LOS VIRREYES MARQUÉS DE CAÑETE Y CONDE DE NIEVA

I

Ni la tragedia de Saxahuamán, en que se levantó el cadalso para el *muy magnífico* D. Gonzalo Pizarro y su bravo maese de campo Francisco de Carbajal, ni el sangriento fin del capitán Francisco Girón, ahorcado algunos años después en la plaza de Lima, alcanzaron á extinguir en el virreinato los motivos de civil discordia. En todos los pueblos del Perú existían dispersos y prontos á ponerse en combustión, tan luego como apareciese un hombre audaz y con sobrada inteligencia para darles dirección, infinitos elementos de anarquía.

Carlos V, en vísperas de encerrarse ya en el monasterio de Yuste y en vista de los circunstanciados informes que recibió de las colonias, llegó á convencerse del peligro en que estaba de perder con el Perú el más bello florón de su corona. Para conjurar la amenazadora tormenta, confirió amplios poderes á D. Andrés Hurtado de Mendoza, marqués de Cañete, y el título de virrey que el conde de Casa Palma no había querido admitir. No se engañó el monarca en la elección de su representante, de quien dice un concienzudo historiador que unía la prudencia de Gasca á la entereza de Blasco Núñez de Vela.

Fig. 7. Nicanor Vásquez Ubach, Illustration for *A prediction fulfilled (the death of the count of Nieva)*. Woodcut on paper. In Ricardo Palma, *Tradiciones peruanas* (Barcelona: Montaner y Simón, 1893). Biblioteca Nacional del Perú, Lima.

Ilustración Peruana

Nota morisca de Lima

Fig. 8. Teófilo Castillo, *A Moorish note in Lima. The tower of La Concepción*. Trichrome reproduction. In *Ilustración peruana* 113 (November 29, 1911). Biblioteca Manuel Solari Swayne, Museo de Arte de Lima.

large Spanish presses, capable of dealing with the different aspects of publishing, from the production of the book as a refined object of consumption to its international distribution. Published by Montaner y Simón, the *Tradiciones peruanas* was illustrated for the first time with small vignettes by the Catalan illustrator Nicanor Vásquez Ubach (1861–1930), who sought to give these images a certain local specificity by including portraits of historical figures, as well as types and scenes drawn from Lima's *costumbrista* tradition (fig. 7). As he lacked visual references to illustrate most of the stories, he dressed Palma's characters in the garb of Spanish images of the Golden Age under the Hapsburgs, a sort of popular Hispanism that had little to do with Iberian history and even less with that of Latin America. Palma's stories were thus initially associated with a broad visual horizon of generic evocations of the Spanish past, a true mass culture that the *Tradiciones peruanas* themselves helped to popularize and maintain. As conventional as they were, the images of swashbucklers and Golden Age characters deployed by Vásquez became historically useful for evoking the legendary opulence of the Peruvian viceroyalty, which had reached its climax precisely in the sixteenth and seventeenth centuries.

However, creating a plausible representation of that local past for a modern audience also required translating the notion of wealth into the terms of a bourgeois consumer culture. This explains why the growing fascination with the colonial past promoted by Palma ended up taking on the appearance of another powerful visual corpus of the European past, current even in Spain itself. Indeed, the stagings of a Frenchified eighteenth century were already a recurring theme in international academic painting and commercial visual culture, as demonstrated by the Peruvian painters Daniel Hernández (1856–1932) and Albert Lynch (1851–after 1900). They had made their fame in official European circuits by producing—as if an inseparable whole—eighteenth-century reconstructions and scenes of modern elegant life, in what was a rather transparent demonstration that their images of the past actually spoke of the present.

Both because of their Peruvian origin and their conservative academic training, Hernández and Lynch would be important references for Teófilo Castillo (1857–1922; fig. 8), the painter who, in the first two decades of the twentieth century, would place that Versaillesque rhetoric in the service of a local heritage. Like his two colleagues, Castillo was trained in Europe, although he returned to Peru in 1905 after an extended stay in Buenos Aires.[21] A perceptive critic, he was well-informed of what was happening in official international circuits, but he also promoted the emergence of a programmatically "Peruvian" art through the reconstruction of the country's artistic past. The different meanings of the term "tradition" would articulate his diverse facets as critic and painter. Because of his interest in the representation of local themes and subjects, he sought to establish a line of continuity with the work of Francisco Laso (1823–1869), the first European-trained Peruvian painter who sought to create national images. In turn, Castillo was a profound admirer of contemporary academic Spanish art, from where he also derived a particular taste for the anecdotal evocation of the past.[22] This inspiration also allowed him to achieve, from Lima, a prominent place within a generation of academic painters who, like Hernández and Lynch, had made their reputations in Europe.

Although Castillo rarely drew directly from *Tradiciones peruanas*, he took on the challenge of creating the definitive visual counterpart of Palma's literary evocations. The artist could thus appeal to a historical imaginary broadly shared

Fig. 9. Teófilo Castillo, *The death of the count of Nieva*, 1918. Oil on canvas, 55⅛ × 13⅜ in. (140 × 34 cm). Museo Central, Banco Central de Reserva del Perú.

Fig. 10. Teófilo Castillo, *Funerals of Saint Rose*, 1918. Oil on canvas, 39 × 80⅜ in. (99 × 204 cm). Museo de Arte de Lima. Donación Memoria Prado.

by a wide reading public, the only significant audience he could count on in a context lacking a true artistic scene. The success of his work, certainly, was not to be played out in an official academic circuit or in the sphere of art criticism, two realms practically nonexistent in Lima at the beginning of the twentieth century. His main site of validation would be the illustrated press, a truly dynamic space of cultural creation that Castillo joined upon his return to Lima. Displaced as a caricaturist with the irruption of more modern aesthetics, the artist maintained his presence in Lima's magazines through the reproduction of many of his paintings, especially small sketches of traditional urban retreats (fig. 8).[23] Symptomatically, even his most ambitious historical evocations, which he largely did not reproduce in magazines, not only assumed formats that emulated the graphic resources of the illustrated press but their unsubtle palette also seemed to evoke the visual effects of the tricolor process used in printing magazines (fig. 9).

Although academic practice did allow licenses to be taken when representing the past, reinforcing verisimilitude at the expense of historical truth, Castillo had to construct a credible fiction of the viceregal past for an audience uninterested in accuracy. His most effective strategy was to insert recognizable fragments taken from various periods of the local past into a conventional image of the eighteenth century that had already been internationally codified. In works such as *Funerales de Santa Rosa* (Funeral of Saint Rose) painted in 1918, he depicts a fictitious but convincing local architectural setting composed of real elements taken from different buildings (fig. 10). The same strategy allows him to represent a gentleman dressed in eighteenth-century French fashion along with a tapada whose skirt and mantle in fact belonged to the Republican period, according to information Palma provided in his *Tradiciones peruanas*. Bound by the logic of pastiche, Castillo's urban scenes would repeatedly evoke the image of Torre Tagle Palace which, as mentioned above, was a rather exceptional construction in Lima's urban context, as the artist himself noted when he claimed that "over four centuries of viceregal and republican rule nothing like it has been produced, not even with the guano and saltpeter millions."[24] By multiplying its presence, the palace convincingly constructed the ideal of a viceregal Lima in which "everything costs a fortune," as Castillo claimed in speaking of the building.[25] It is even more symptomatic that the universe of actual viceregal objects had no place in this selective representation of the past. This was evidenced by works such as the *El santo de la abuelita* (The grandmother's birthday), the setting of which actually evokes the bourgeois taste for historical, industrially produced, French-style furniture (fig. 11).

With his pictorial work, Castillo created an imaginary of colonial Lima that complemented Palma's literary evocations and was just as powerful as them. In effect, he laid the foundations for the definition of a true local mass culture that would revolve around a paradoxically timeless viceregal Lima, in which different historical eras intertwined to articulate a unified repertoire of clichés. Through the diffuse profiles of loose brushstrokes, his colonial fictions seemed to emerge, literally, from the mists of time. At the same time, they revealed all their modernity by projecting onto the viceroyalty that material abundance that characterized bourgeois interiors, by then established as the true sign of material progress (fig. 12).

The Logic of Excess

Castillo not only constructed his colonial evocations on the inspiration of academic painting, but, as Fernando Villegas points out, he also

Above: Fig. 11. Teófilo Castillo, *The Grandmother's Birthday*, ca. 1917. Oil on canvas, 39 × 52⅜ in. (99.1 × 133 cm). Museo de Arte de Lima: Donación Luis Solari Swayne y Hortensia Romero Solari.

Below: Fig. 12. Teófilo Castillo, *Coquetry*. Trichrome reproduction. In *Ilustración Peruana* 111 (November 15, 1911): 113. Biblioteca Manuel Solari Swayne, Museo de Arte de Lima.

Fig. 13. Adolphe Dubreuil, *Characters from "El santo de la abuelita" posing at the Torre Tagle Palace*, 1917. In *Mundial* (July 28, 1921). Biblioteca Manuel Solari Swayne, Museo de Arte de Lima.

seems to have been inspired by the work of the American traveler C. L. Chester, photographer and correspondent for foreign publications known for his albums of views of the Peruvian capital and the central highlands produced for travelers passing through Peru.[26] Around 1910, Chester made several photographic records of Torre Tagle, where, in Castillo's words, he sought to capture "the soul of the colonial era, evoking it by means of living human models, representing lavish viceregal scenes."[27] In 1924, a little over a decade later, he founded Pictoria del Peru, a film company established to promote abroad, on commission of the Peruvian government, the country's natural resources and "progress."[28] This partnership brings new light to Aracy Amaral's argument on the importance of the relationship between the emergence of Neocolonial styles and the impact of historicisms deployed in cinematographic architecture and in American culture more generally.[29]

In fact, the true success of the Neocolonial style as a construction of national identity could only be achieved through a mass culture that soon pervaded different aspects of modern life. The impact of those Versaillesque evocations

Fig. 14. Diego Goyzueta, *Portrait of an Unidentified Woman*, ca. 1925–30. Gelatin silver print. Collection of Luis Eduardo Wuffarden, Lima, Peru.

of the viceregal past was felt in 1917, with the celebrations for the three hundredth anniversary of the death of Saint Rose of Lima. Lima's elite then gathered at the capital's Excelsior Theater to attend the staging of *El santo de la abuelita*, an anecdotal theatrical representation set in colonial times. The actors, who also belonged to the city's so-called elegant society, took advantage of their costumes to pose for a session with photographer Adolphe Dubreuil at the Torre Tagle Palace, where they recreated Castillo's Lima (fig. 13). In the words of an anonymous newspaper editor, the highlight of that performance had been the

magnificent and splendid reproduction of viceregal Lima in the eighteenth century. A perfect and exact expression of court life of that time. A party was being held at the house of the Duchess of San Carlos, who was celebrating her birthday. On that occasion, they entered the salon, magnificently furnished with admirably carved furniture, with a beautiful viceregal dais in the background. Invited to play the harpsichord by the owners of the house upon the arrival of the viceroy, Count of Superunda, the Countess of Laura, represented by the beautiful Carmen Ortiz de Zevallos y del Solar, played with admirable mastery some delicate and simple airs of distant times, which surely delighted our grandparents.[30]

An accumulation of decontextualized references to the past sustained the false illusion of truth. As in *Un litigio original* (An original lawsuit), a famous Palma *tradición* that contains a long enumeration of local titles of nobility, twenty-four of the actors in *El santo de la abuelita* took on the roles of dukes, counts, and marquises.[31] The resulting images gained greater prominence in 1921, when they reappeared in the reports published by the press on occasion of the centennial of Peru's independence, to the point that other Lima photographers produced similar images. The most daring of the latter would be Diego Goyzueta, who would use cinematographic cues to photograph his wealthiest clientele in vague historical environments that could simultaneously evoke both colonial times and late eighteenth-century France (fig. 14).[32]

That imprecise way of evoking the past had also marked the strategy deployed by the Peruvian state in the context of the celebrations of the centennial of independence from Spain. An organic narrative placed the origins of the Peruvian nation in an immemorial prehispanic past, while the viceroyalty appeared as the key moment of Westernization, marking the entry of Peru into the order of so-called civilized nations. Far from alluding to the violence that characterized the wars against the Spanish crown, the official narrative aimed to describe independence as the moment when the country had reached a sort of coming of age that allowed it to be *emancipated* from the Mother Country, as Spain came to be called. Only allegory could give a transcendent appearance to this type of anecdotal evocation of the colonial past and of a supposedly timeless "Hispanicity," whose visual icons were rather modern and had no real relation to local history. Nowhere is this clearer than in *El paso de los libertadores*, an ambitious composition that presided over the hall destined to receive the foreign delegations attending the festivities (fig. 15). Painted by Hernández, who had returned to Peru to direct the recently created National School of Fine Arts, this work does not represent any real historic event. It shows the improbable parade of the leaders of the liberating armies before a motley crowd which prominently included a group of *manolas*, Spanish *costumbrista* types that did not exist in Lima's older visual culture.

Fig. 15. Daniel Hernández, *The Liberator's Parade*, 1924. Oil on canvas, 17 ft. 4⅝ in. × 14 ft. 6 in. (530 × 442 cm). Benemérita Sociedad Fundadores de la Independencia, Lima.

Hernández's large painting was one of the many state commissions for the celebrations of the Centennial of Independence. In a country that seemed to be on the road to progress thanks to economic growth generated by an export boom and dependence on US loans, many of the historical colonial monuments seemed insufficient to symbolize that grandiose past necessary to cement Peru as a modern nation. As the critic Juan de Zavaleta unambiguously pointed out, noting the contrast between the historic city center prior to its modernization and the legend created by Palma: "Whoever visited Lima twenty or twenty-five years ago and saw it possessed of these general suggestions would have reason to feel truly deceived."[33] The spectacular nature of cinematic architecture seemed to be reflected in the ambitious urban projects proposed by the Polish architect Bruno Paprocki in the late 1920s, whose ambitious perspectives implied a radical break with the colonial layout of the city (fig. 16).[34] In that context, the art critic Carlos Solari went so far as to propose replacing the original materials of the city's most important colonial facades with cement to give them the noble appearance of stone (the list would have included the facade of the palace of Torre Tagle, with its stucco decorations).[35] As if it were a game of mirrors that made it impossible to distinguish between the original and the copy, Solari must have had in his memory the archbishop's palace, a sort of Beaux Arts version of Torre Tagle built in concrete three years earlier by architects Ricardo de la Jaxa Malachowski (1887–1972) and Claudio Sahut (1883–1932; figs. 17 and 18). The critic himself lived in one of the new concrete evocations of viceregal architecture, which seemed to lend true corporeality to a colonial Lima that had previously only unfolded in literary or pictorial fictions. The growing irruption of

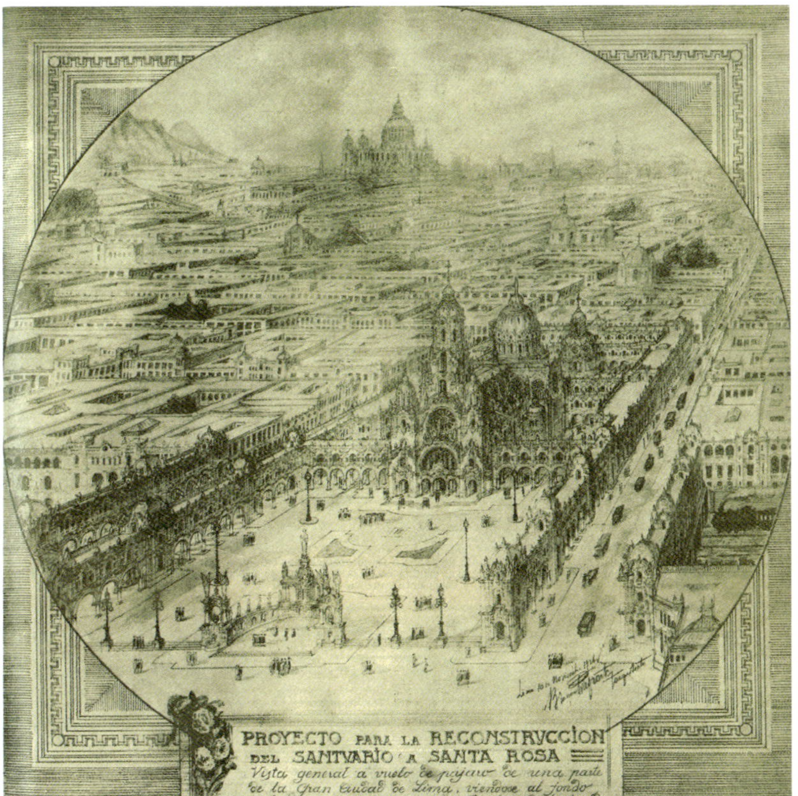

Fig. 16. Bruno Paprocki, *Project for the reconstruction of the Sanctuary of Saint Rose of Lima*. In *Mundial* (Lima) 7 (November 26, 1926): 337. Biblioteca Manuel Solari Swayne, Museo de Arte de Lima.

Above: Fig. 17. Ricardo de la Jaxa Malachowski, Palace of the Archbishopric, Lima, Peru, 1924. Photograph courtesy of the author.

Right: Fig. 18. Facade of Torre Tagle Palace, Lima, Peru, built ca. 1738. Postcard, 1920s. Photograph courtesy the author.

the Neocolonial style in the capital's architecture was called to fill that gap. In 1921, the Bolivarian Museum opened in the so-called Quinta de la Magdalena, a simple colonial recreational house to which a striking baroque facade was added, in a style largely shaped by the expectations of the new popular imagination of viceregal art. In a paradoxical turn, that museum was dedicated to the memories of those who fought against the Spanish crown in the wars of independence.

The gulf separating the colonial past and the selective memory of the modern nation became much wider as it entered everyday life. As symbols of local identity and elements of social prestige, colonial objects were in demand beyond specialized or elite collecting, finding their ways into the domestic interiors of a growing middle class.[36] But their relationship with modern fictions of the colonial past had limits. In the first place, the most valued pieces were scarce and insufficient to satisfy a demand that also included a nascent tourist market. Secondly, few representations recorded the much admired daily or festive life of the viceroyalty. If the viceregal period could be described—in the words of José de la Riva Agüero—as "a great convent, with its sleepy stillness, its monotony interrupted by pompous festivities," history was linked to names more than to transcendental historical events.[37]

And if anecdote was the main modern form of imagining the colonial past, the succession of royal personages that gave it historical legitimacy also had no direct relationship with most paintings, sculptures, or antique furniture still in existence. This void would be filled by a novel industry of evocation, which serially produced complete sets of portraits of viceroys and archbishops, kings, queens, and furnishings of all kinds.

Fig. 19. Conservation process revealing colonial image of a saint overpainted with a portrait of Charles IV and his family. Restoration workshop of the Museo Pedro de Osma, Lima.

In the dynamics of excess, objects from all eras could be recycled, intermingled whole or deployed as fragments. It can certainly be argued that these were common practices among the less scrupulous antique dealers around the world. In the Lima market, however, the dominant tendency was not to imitate what was known without a doubt to be colonial. Rather, it was a matter of creating absolutely new images that would meet the expectations of commonplaces that either had no real counterpart in the actual material culture of the colonial era or evoked forms lost as a result of the convulsive history of the region. A viceregal court could not be imagined without its distant kings, and yet such images were exceptional in the colonial painting that had been preserved. What is telling is that even those portraits that did exist also failed to meet the expectations of Versaillesian "glamour" that modern viewers assigned to European court life. The factory of evocations, however, was able to make up for those demands by multiplying representations of whatever royal lineage was required. Such is the case of an ingenious pastiche based on a fragment of the famous portrait of Philip V's family by Louis Michel Van Loo. The canvas is painted over a viceregal Cuzco canvas, one of the many religious images transformed by the antiquarian trade (fig. 19).

As colonial opulence seemed to be summed up in the gleam of rich gilt carving, producers of antiques would go so far as to create improbable frames full of false carved details, which were actually made of molded plaster and mirrors. As in the paintings of Teófilo Castillo, original fragments from different periods were brought together in unusual objects, whose main merit was to give validity to that fictitious viceregal past admired by their owners. The play of mirrors between the original and the copy thus ended up creating a hypertrophic image of the past.

This is the case of the gigantic balconies of the Plaza Mayor, designed by Emilio Hart-Terré in the 1940s (see fig. 18). Undoubtedly, as Horacio Ramos suggests, despite their emphatic ornamentation, those works marked the search for a local response to the challenge posed by the growing prestige of international architectural modernism.[38] But the Neocolonial had always been an attempt to reconcile the elusive and ever-changing nature of progress with the "identity of the nation," which, though claiming to be timeless, was evidently a modern creation. For the same reason, if the theatrical productions of the 1940s shunned the decorative excesses of the plays presented twenty years earlier, the actors still belonged to the local elite, so they represented, in the garb of the past, their privileged situation in the present. But with the power of a true mass culture anchored in the very origins of local modernity, that fanciful viceregal Lima would be capable of assimilating everything, even a radically republican popular culture, as Sebastián Salazar Bondy ironically pointed out when denouncing the tendentious exaltation of a fictitious past through an absolutely illusory colonial Arcadia, in which "it is not easy to prove that in the taverns or orchards of seventeenth-century Lima *anticuchos* were served, *polkitas* were danced, nor that the guests were entertained with pisco or chicha."[39]

In 1958, when functionalist modernism had already won the battle against neocolonial architecture, those modern fictions of the viceroyalty showed their full validity in the exhibition organized in Paris by the Peruvian government. Presented at the Petit Palais, the exhibition *The Treasures of Peru* included several supposedly colonial objects with an evidently modern appearance. It was considered, however, that their authenticity was certified by the presence of inscriptions that related them to important historical characters, as if the material culture of the colonial period were but a reflection of Ricardo Palma's evocative anecdotes. What surprised the French press the most was that the shipment included a Saint Joan of Arc that supposedly dated to the eighteenth century.[40] Although its owner, collector Pedro de Osma, was probably not aware of the obvious forgery, it is also likely that he considered the work as an anachronistic, but necessary, wink to attract the attention of the Parisian public. Osma was not alone. Even today, in the intimacy of many domestic spaces, implausible objects of all kinds continue to sustain a shared fiction: that of the pretend antiquity of an imaginary produced by modernity. As from the beginning of the twentieth century, the Neocolonial style was there to cover the absences of the past that prevented Peru from being recognized as a modern nation in the present.

Notes

1. José de la Riva Agüero, "Nuestras iglesias (fragmento de la introducción a un estudio sobre los cronistas de convento)," *Prisma* 3, no. 49 (July 28, 1907): 9.

2. *Recuerdo de la inauguración del templo de San Agustín* (Lima, Peru: Imprenta de E. Moreno, 1908), 45.

3. Riva Agüero, "Nuestras iglesias," 9. Unless otherwise noted, all translations from the Spanish by the author.

4. Ibid.

5. José de la Riva Agüero, *Carácter de la literatura del Perú Independiente* (Lima, Peru: E. Rosay Editor, 1905).

6. See Riva Agüero, *Carácter de la literatura del Perú Independiente*, 249.

7. Ibid., 152.

8. Ibid.

9. Ibid., 154.

10. See Natalia Majluf, *La creación del costumbrismo: las acuarelas de la donación Juan Carlos Verme* (Lima, Peru: MALI, Museo de Arte de Lima; IFEA, Instituto Francés de Estudios Andinos, 2016), 4–33.

11. See "La tradición de la saya y manto," in Ricardo Palma, *Apéndice a mis últimas tradiciones peruanas* (Barcelona: Editorial Maucci, 1910), 49–54.

12. Manuel Lorenzo de Vidaurre, "Congreso: discurso pronunciado por el Sr. Vidaurre, sobre la proposición del Sr. Rodriguez, relativa á que se impida introducir por extranjeros las cosas, que pueden trabajarse, fabricarse, y recojerse en el país," *El Conciliador* (Lima) 3, no. 13 (February 15, 1832): [3].

13. Ibid.

14. "El baile de la Victoria," in Palma, *Apéndice a mis últimas tradiciones peruanas*, 87–98.

15. Paul Rizo-Patrón Boylan, *Linaje, dote y poder: la nobleza de Lima de 1700 a 1830* (Lima, Peru: Fondo Editorial de la PUCP, 2000), 263–65.

16. Ricardo Palma, *Peru: tradiciones* (Lima, Peru: Imprenta de Carlos Prince, 1883).

17. Javier Prado y Ugarteche, *Estado Social del Perú durante la dominación española* (Lima, Peru: Imprenta de El Diario Judicial, 1894), 142–43.

18. Mariela Mondragón, "La mirada crítica de Ricardo Palma sobre el aspecto gráfico de sus *Tradiciones peruanas* (1872-1897)," *Yuyaykusun* (Lima), no. 10 (2020): 33–53.

19. Diana Arbaiza, *The Spirit of Hispanism: Commerce, Culture, and Identity across the Atlantic, 1875–1936* (Notre Dame, IN: University of Notre Dame Press, 2020).

20. Ricardo Palma, *Tradiciones peruanas*, 4 vols. (Barcelona: Montaner y Simón, 1893–1896).

21. Fernando Villegas Torres, *El Perú a través de la pintura y crítica de Teófilo Castillo (1887-1922: nacionalismo, modernización y nostalgia en la Lima del 900* (Lima, Peru: Asamblea Nacional de Rectores, 2006), 161–64.

22. Fernando Villegas Torres, *Vínculos artísticos entre España y el Perú (1892-1929): elementos para la construcción del imaginario nacional peruano* (Lima: Fondo Editorial del Congreso del Perú, 2016), 30–31.

23. Ricardo Kusunoki Rodríguez, "El arte fuera del arte. Una historia de lo moderno en fragmentos (Perú, 1900-1940)," in *Arte y Tesoros del Perú, 50 años, nuevas miradas*, ed. Ramón Mujica Pinilla (Lima: Banco de Crédito del Perú, 2023), 280–303.

24. Teófilo Castillo, "Interiores Limeños. X. Casa del Doctor Ricardo Ortiz de Zevallos (Sucesión de los Marqueses de Torre-Tagle)," *Variedades* (Lima) 10, no. 366 (March 6, 1915): 1854.

25. Ibid.

26. Villegas, *El Perú a través de la pintura y crítica de Teófilo Castillo (1887-1922)*, 111; C. L. Chester, *Lima: descripción pintoresca de la Ciudad Capital del Perú* (Lima, Peru: editada exclusivamente para Edw. Muecke, [1913]).

27. Teófilo Castillo, "El arte fotográfico en Lima," *Variedades* (Lima) 10, no. 345 (October 10, 1914): 1306.

28. *Memoria que el Ministro de Fomento, Ing.º D. Manuel G. Masias, presenta al Congreso Extraordinario de 1924* (Lima, Peru: Casa Editorial La Opinión Nacional, 1925), 39–40.

29. Aracy Amaral, "La invención de un pasado," in *Arquitectura neocolonial: América Latina, Caribe, Estados Unidos*, ed. Aracy Amaral (São Paulo: Fondo de Cultura Económica, 1994), 11–16.

30. *Recuerdo de las Fiestas del Tercer Centenario de la Muerte de Santa Rosa de Lima* (Lima, Peru: Imp. Artística, 1917), 131–32.

31. Palma, *Tradiciones peruanas*, vol. 1 (Barcelona: Montaner y Simón, 1893), 58–68; *Recuerdo de las Fiestas*, 134–35.

32. Antonio Garland, "El arte eximio de Diego Goyzueta," *Variedades* (Lima), no. 940 (March 7, 1926), n.p.

33. Juan de Zavaleta, "El renacimiento de la arquitectura colonial de Lima," *Mundial* (Lima) 3, no. 103 (May 5, 1922): n.p.

34. On Paprocky's projects, see"Basílica á Santa Rosa," *Mundial* (Lima), 7, no. 332 (October 22, 1926): n.p.; "Un bello proyecto arquitectónico," *Mundial* (Lima) 8, no. 363 (May 27, 1927): n.p.; "De arte: los proyectos de Paprocki," *Mundial* (Lima) 8, no. 377 (September 2, 1927): n.p.

35. Don Quijote [Carlos Solari], "Un ejemplo concluyente," *Mundial* (Lima) 8, no. 377 (September 2, 1927): n.p.

36. See "Sólo para mujeres: la adaptación de los muebles coloniales," *Mundial* (Lima) 10, no. 502 (February 1, 1930): n.p.

37. José de la Riva Agüero, *La historia en el Perú* (PhD dissertation, Imprenta Nacional de Federico Barrionuevo, 1910), 220.

38. Horacio Ramos Cerna, "Destrucción y reinvención de la Plaza de Armas de Lima, 1924-1954" (master's thesis, Pontificia Universidad Católica del Perú, 2015).

39. Sebastián Salazar Bondy, *Lima la horrible* (Mexico City: Ediciones Era, 1964), 21.

40. Raymond Charmet, "El Perú moderno ha vuelto a encontrar un arte original e inventivo," *Cultura Peruana* (Lima), no. 121 (July 1958): n.p.

CARLA GUILLERMINA GARCÍA

Martín Noel: Cultural Routes and Pictorial Maps

Architect Martín Noel (1888–1963) arises as an indisputable leader in the Neocolonial movement that recovered and promoted architecture to establish Latin American identity. Inspired by the Neocolonial style in the Americas and Europe, Noel designed Argentina's pavilion in the Ibero-American Exposition in Seville, a paradigmatic example of the period (fig.1). Commissioned by President Marcelo Torcuato de Alvear, the architect brought to life "a viceregal style, characterized by the fusion of American art and the Spanish Renaissance."[1] Also important were his roles as a Hispanic American architectural historian and as a cultural manager within governmental institutions, in particular, at the Academia Nacional de Bellas Artes (National Academy of Fine Arts) founded in Buenos Aires in 1936, where he served as president for almost twenty years.

The recovery of Hispanic American art in Argentina at the beginning of the twentieth century occurred in a specific context that intellectual historians named "centennial spirit."[2] The expression was coined by José Luis Romero to put into words a social and intellectual transformation that found its symbolic expression during the Centennial of the May Revolution

Fig. 1. Martín Noel at Argentina's pavilion at the Exposición Iberoamericana, Seville, Spain, 1929. Archivo General de la Nación, Argentina, Departamento de Documentos Fotográficos.

celebration in 1910. In this context, Hispanism gained prominence as an ideological current, along with a reconsideration of the peninsular heritage as an alternative to the liberal tradition of the nineteenth century. Ricardo Rojas, the most influential Argentine cultural historian of the beginning of the century, wrote *Eurindia* in 1924, in which he laid the foundations of an approach to aesthetics that focused on the concept of cultural fusion with the aim of considering the exchange between Spain and America through the exaltation of the virtues from Hispanic and Indigenous *mestizaje*.[3]

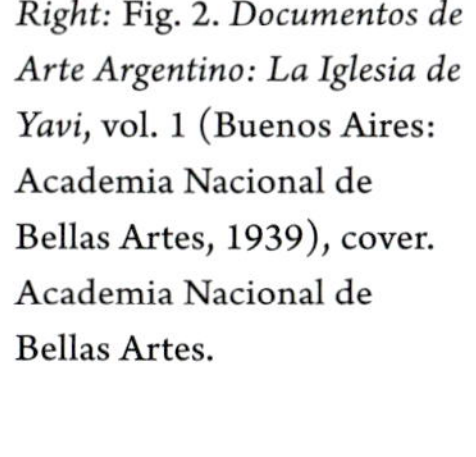

Right: Fig. 2. *Documentos de Arte Argentino: La Iglesia de Yavi*, vol. 1 (Buenos Aires: Academia Nacional de Bellas Artes, 1939), cover. Academia Nacional de Bellas Artes.

Below: Fig. 3. Church of Rinconada, Jujuy. Photograph by Hans Mann, in *Documentos de Arte Argentino: Por la ruta de los Inkas y en la Quebrada de Humahuaca*, vol. 3 (Buenos Aires: Academia Nacional de Bellas Artes 1940), 47.

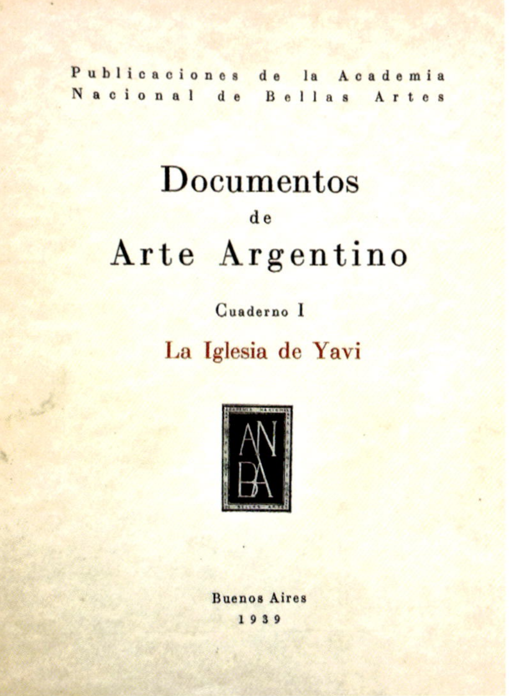

Publicaciones de la Academia Nacional de Bellas Artes

Documentos de Arte Argentino

Cuaderno I

La Iglesia de Yavi

ANBA

Buenos Aires

1939

The interest in the colonial past, which originated in the context of cultural nationalism during the Centennial, was consolidated in the following decades when historians, encouraged by the conservative government to settle in Argentina, began working for the state after the coup in 1930.[4] The intention was to awaken an emotional attachment to the nation, and historical monuments, naturally, played a significant role in this awakening. At the II° Congreso Internacional de Historia de América (Second International Congress of American History) held in Buenos Aires in 1937, the main figures of Hispanic American art gathered on that occasion: Manuel Toussaint of Mexico, José Gabriel Navarro of Ecuador, José Uriel García of Peru, and Martín Noel of Argentina. It was the first time that such an event devoted a session to colonial art, and it was the perfect occasion for the session's participants to express two main concerns: the deplorable state of the preservation of architectural and artistic monuments—directly related to a lack of government actions—and the absence of an inventory of buildings and artworks from the viceregal period. While discussing this with his colleagues, Navarro stated: "We do not even keep pictures; on the one hand, we know that many of those art pieces were, in most cases, part of a clandestine emigration or were knowingly relocated, yet we cannot find them. On the other hand, even permanent monuments such as architectural ones are frequently damaged, in more than one occasion by the authorities who show a limited understanding of the matter."[5]

Noel's interests coincided with those of the other session participants. While working as an architect, he also wrote about architecture and collaborated with cultural institutions interested in recovering pictures of past Latin American art. The National Academy was one of those institutions, and it is this aspect of Noel's intellectual profile that I want to focus on: his role as cultural operator in the dissemination of colonial heritage.

The academy's main interest was the development of a project called *Documentos de Arte Argentino*, which was directly linked to the creation of a photographic archive of the "country's artistic treasures" (fig. 2).[6] The collection was published in the form of twenty-five issues between 1939 and 1947, and each included a brief prologue from a guest writer and a separate section of prints with photographs taken by Hans Mann (1902–1966), the institution's official photographer (fig. 3). Mann created a photographic record that was completely original: not only did he rediscover pictures not previously considered for a similar publication, but he also established a model for a specific historical registry that became a distinctive feature of this series and served as a template for the institution's projects for decades.[7]

With the *Documentos de Arte Argentino*, the academy defined an institutional identity, established a highly specific framework for action with respect to other organizations, and set off path-breaking work for the time. Noel was the main project leader in addition to being president of the academy for almost twenty years; thus, separating this institutional project from his own interests is extremely difficult. Moreover, given his political visibility due to his role as national deputy in charge of formulating and promoting a national artistic inventory, Noel spread the academy's work to other official organizations (figs. 4 and 5). On the occasion of the enactment of law N°12.665 concerning the creation of the Comisión Nacional de Museos y Monumentos

La Reparación
HABLA Martín Noel
DON MARTIN NOEL
Las cinco glosas
UNA PREGUNTA INSOSLAYABLE
HORA DE LEVANTAR LA PUNTERIA

Fig. 4. Martín Noel on architecture and urbanism, *La Reparación*, September 27, 1943. Academia Nacional de la Historia, Archivo Martín Noel.

LA PRENSA
LA PUNA
DE ATACAMA
Y LOS VALLES
CALCHAQUIES

Fig.5. Announcement of the Academia Nacional de Bellas Artes's publications about the northwest. *La Prensa*, October 3, 1940. Fundación Espigas.

y Lugares Históricos (National Commission of Museums and Monuments and Historical Sites) in 1938, Noel said:

I must say that the work carried out by the Academia Nacional de Bellas Artes has aimed at formalizing the well-known inventory of that national artistic heritage, given that a collection of documents called "Arte Argentino" was published in order to document, from north to south of our Republic, a series of live elements of our nationality, perfectly defined on its buildings' plastic appearance. Thus, when we associate the architecture's nature with "the face of the nation" as Alberdi said, these powerful and precious elements to our nation arise and join the landscape of our great provinces.[8]

The idea of an artistic topography that could systematically document national monuments scattered "from the far north to the Río de la Plata area" involved traveling across the territory and accessing lesser-known sites, some of them located in ancient towns that were once under the *encomienda* system.[9] The distances covered and travels made by Mann link *Documentos de Arte Argentino* with the modernized road system of a connected country, which had started to consolidate through well-defined governmental policies. In what follows, I consider how the academy's intention to promote Argentine heritage and to determine its importance relate to modernization policies that included the development of a road system and the promotion of national tourism in the 1930s. Additionally, I address how Noel's ideas about architecture and territory affected this relationship.[10]

Heritage Routes

In 1932, with the establishment of the Dirección Nacional de Vialidad (National

Right: Fig. 6. Cover of *Automovilismo* 19, no. 236 (August 1939).

Far right: Fig. 7. Ford advertisement included in *Automovilismo*, no. 219 (May 1938): 37.

Roads Directorate), a national road network was developed for more utilitarian uses, but it had the added effect of encouraging tourism and positioning it as an economic activity. Car tourism became part of a patriotic education that included historical heritage sites among the natural attractions, and the Argentine northwest, in particular, occupied a prominent position as "the cradle of the homeland" and became a much visited area.[11] The relationship between nature and heritage resulted in a model of tourism that became prevalent in this period, "in which landscape and milestones of history and national progress were linked."[12] This model involved a type of driving tourism related to the traveler's freedom to visit multiple sites without a set itinerary, unlike train travel with its scheduled stops.

Magazine covers and advertisements published during this period, such as *Automovilismo*, included illustrations of colonial architecture next to identifiable scenic views: a typical northern temple with atrium, a side tower and a gable roof, and an example of a Jesuit church with a bell tower from Córdoba province (figs. 6 and 7). Here, we can also notice a "montage operation" over the traditional depiction of the Argentine landscape. In both cases, the car and the road that provide access to these sites have been added and in one of them a figure of a modern and fashionable woman who ventures to northern Argentina.[13]

This process of commercialization of cultural sites for tourism found a strong ally in public organizations with the aim of putting a high value on artistic heritage (fig. 8). The Comisión Nacional de Museos y Monumentos y de Lugares Históricos (National Commission of Museums and Monuments and of Historical Places) is a benchmark institution due to the close relationship between its president, Ricardo Levene (1885–1959), political leaders from

AUTOMOVILISMO

MONUMENTOS HISTORICOS DE SANTA FE

La hermosa provincia del litoral argentino posee monumentos históricos de inapreciable valor. En esta nota, cuyo material gráfico ha sido gentilmente cedido por la Comisión Nacional de Museos y de Monumentos y Lugares Históricos, que preside el doctor Ricardo Levene, se exponen algunos de ellos.

Artística verja de hierro forjado en la casa del general Estanislao López.

Imagen del Nazareno, donada al convento de San Francisco por la reina María Ana de Austria.

Fachada del Templo y Convento de San Francisco, en Santa Fe.

La casa habitación de "La Estanzuela" que perteneció al general Echagüe.

Hermosa pieza del arte colonial: Iglesia de la Inmaculada, de la Compañía de Jesús.

AL igual que los demás territorios argentinos, también la provincia de Santa Fe, cuna de preclaros patriotas, conserva con cariñoso celo los monumentos históricos que han de ofrecer a las nuevas generaciones, como un aleccionador recuerdo, la gesta magnífica de los hombres que labraron nuestra argentinidad.

Todo el suelo santafesino ofrece estos ejemplos de tenacidad y patriotismo, residiendo su mayor interés en las construcciones de estilo colonial, en las cuales se conservan verdaderas joyas del arte religioso.

Un ejemplo de ello es el Templo y Convento de San Francisco, cuya construcción data del año 1860, y en cuyo interior se halla enterrado el brigadier general D. Estanislao López. De este prócer se conserva también la casa en la cual vivió y muriera, sita en las calles General López y 9 de Julio.

Otro monumento celosamente conservado es La Estanzuela, casa de campo de extraordinario valor arquitectónico, edificada a comienzos del siglo XIX, y que sirvió de residencia campestre al ex gobernador don Pascual Echagüe.

El Templo de la Merced, o Templo de la Inmaculada, que perteneció a la Compañía de Jesús, es el edificio más antiguo de Santa Fe, ya que data del año 1660. Se venera allí la Imagen de los Milagros, el más antiguo óleo colonial pintado en el país, que se atribuye a los Hermanos Verges.

Se conserva allí también un trozo de claustro y habitaciones primitivas que ocuparon los constituyentes de 1853.

PARA EL SEGURO DE SU AUTOMOVIL CONSULTE A
LA UNION MERCANTIL
COMPAÑIA DE SEGUROS
FUNDADA EN 1901
OFICINAS EN EL EDIFICIO DE SU PROPIEDAD
RIVADAVIA 540 • BUENOS AIRES • U. T. 33-4441

Fig. 8. "Monumentos historicos de Santa Fe," with pictures provided by the National Comission of Museums and Monuments, *Automovilismo*, no. 265 (May–April 1942): n.p.

that period, and the Automobile Club members who had participated in making the Ley Nacional de Vialidad, a law that established road development in national territory.[14] Within this context, the academy played a less direct role; it was committed to the dissemination of heritage by means of its long-term editorial project and not necessarily advertising to the tourist trade. Because it prioritized the creation of its own archive, the production and dissemination of its images was limited. Also, the format of *Documentos de Arte Argentino* established a privileged connection with cultural and economic interests of the period as a sort of final product that combined the attention for past artistic images with the landscape of the provinces.

Mann's journeys through the country to create a historical registry were a major concern for the academy due to the resources necessary for traveling and his photographic equipment, so the road development that started in the 1930s was crucial to the academy's project. Because the first issues were dedicated to northern provinces, featuring hardly accessible remote towns, the academy decided to acquire a car in order for Mann to travel more easily to Salta and Jujuy provinces.[15] These initial journeys made Mann an essential mediator. Because the prologue writers were not able to work *in situ*, they used his pictures to write each issue. But his photos were also crucial for the social imaginary based on the desire to have both an integrated and a heterogeneous country, a country whose highly diverse regions were well connected.

Fig. 9. Detail of belfry and porch, church of Yavi. Photograph by Hans Mann. *Documentos de Arte Argentino: la Iglesia de Yavi*, vol. 1 (Buenos Aires: Academia Nacional de Bellas Artes, 1939), 6. Academia Nacional de Bellas Artes.

Maps and Pictures

I will come back to Mann's pictures, but first I want to address the correlation between the first issues dedicated to northern Argentina and Noel's historiographical program. In his prologues about the province of Jujuy that opened the collection, and more specifically in the modest architectural aspect of Yavi—the church to which the first issue is dedicated—Noel emphasizes the characteristics of a rustic architecture typical of the region and connects it with the artistic traditions of Upper Peru. He refers to it as "the traveling church of Yavi" and underlines that, because of its location bordering Bolivia, migrant artists were able to leave their mark on the Argentine northwest (fig. 9).[16]

Noel identifies a model characteristic of the region's tradition when comparing the church's structure with other churches that have one nave and a lateral tower; therefore, the church at Yavi represents a landmark that denotes the first production, the consolidation of a prototype, and the popularity of this model in other provinces. As Jorge Tomasi argues, Noel considered it an early testimony of church architecture and a "pristine source of inspiration" in order to define an authentic national architecture.[17] As Noel explained:

Hence the particular interest in recording examples such as the encomienda church of Yavi, which, although modest, in the solitude of the surrounding landscape, it awakens the primary ascendant of our first steps into the world of art; so much so that when its noisy doors are opened, we will discover the unsuspected treasure of its rich ornamentation and this, more than the church's naïve facade, will completely reveal to us the prestige of that "Ibero-Andean" style that was the artistic crucible of our creole world.[18]

The Andean region as a source of local artistic development is associated with certain values that are the starting point to consider what national heritage represents in Noel's speech. These values prioritize Indigenous elements and features from the architecture and artworks of the great cultures that thrived before the Spanish arrived and so connect these northern churches with the idea of an American antiquity. It is in the interior of the temple, richly decorated, where Noel discovers a buried treasure (figs. 10 and 11). The opulent decorations lead him to postulate miscellaneous influences—the quality of sculptural works on the retable and pulpit recall Cuzco, and the dramatic elements in the imagery suggest Seville—but a certain strictly American strength—that he sees as an "archaic purpose"—is added.[19]

Noel's approach, focused on the concept of fusion and cultural mestizaje, rapidly diminishes the distinctive features of the American

Left: Fig. 10. "View of chancel with its two altars and of the trapezoidal framing, church of Yavi." Photograph by Hans Mann. *Documentos de Arte Argentino: la Iglesia de Yavi*, vol. 1 (Buenos Aires: Academia Nacional de Bellas Artes, 1939), 11. Academia Nacional de Bellas Artes.

Right: Fig. 11. "St. John the Baptist a noble image seen from a niche on the high altar. Reveals clearly influences of the Seville-Granada school." Photograph by Hans Mann. *Documentos de Arte Argentino: la Iglesia de Yavi*, vol. 1 (Buenos Aires: Academia Nacional de Bellas Artes, 1939), 14. Academia Nacional de Bellas Artes.

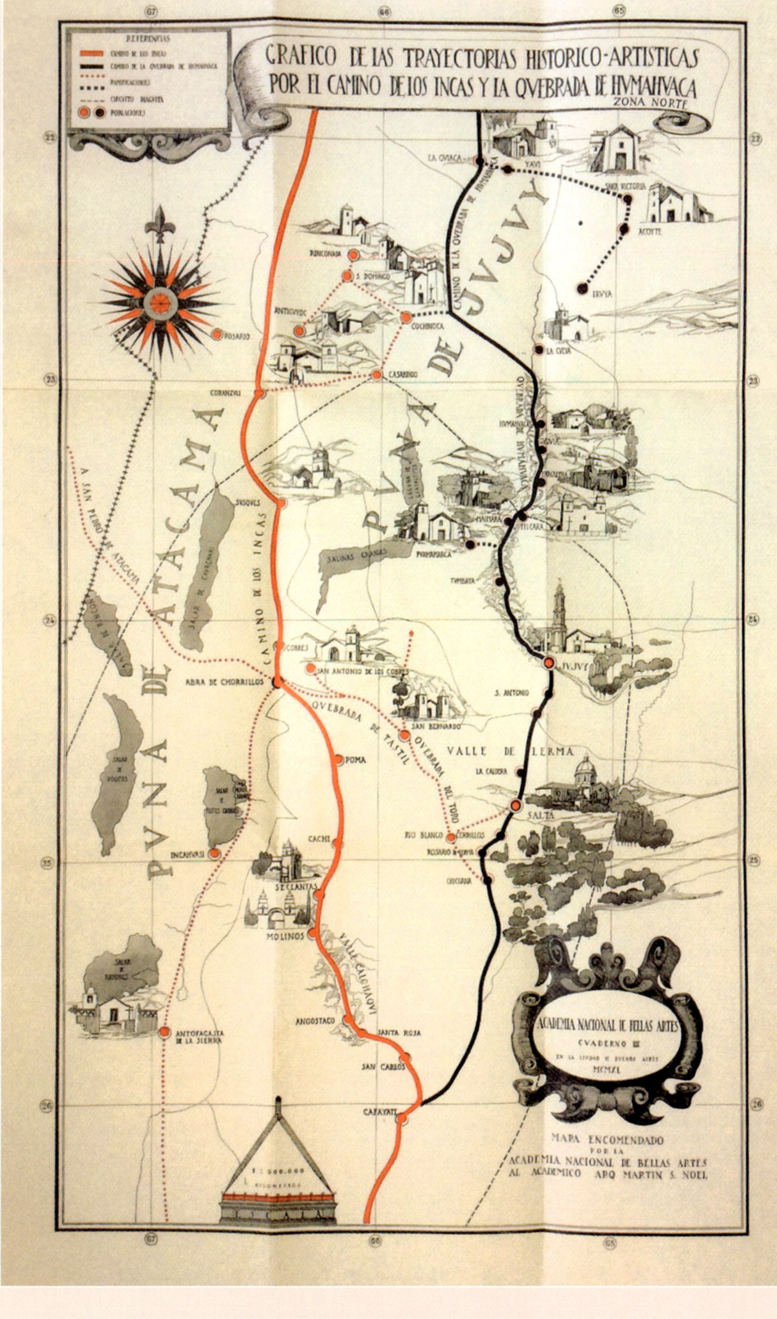

Fig. 12. Map by Martín Noel, "Graphic of the historical-artistic trajectories along the Camino de los Incas and the Quebrada de Humahuaca." *Documentos de Arte Argentino: Por la ruta de los Inkas y en la Quebrada de Humahuaca*, vol. 3 (Buenos Aires: Academia Nacional de Bellas Artes, 1940), n.p. Academia Nacional de Bellas Artes.

Fig. 13. Map of Ciudad de Cordoba by Jorge Lima and Raúl Repetto for the IV Salón Nacional de Arquitectura. *Revista de Arquitectura* 27, no. 268 (April 1943): [162]. Academia Nacional de Bellas Artes.

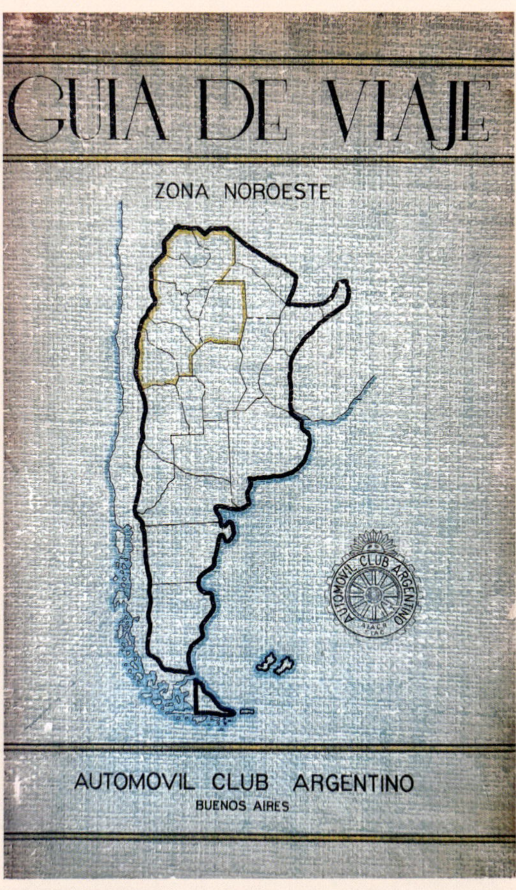

Fig. 14. Cover of *Guía de viaje: zona noroeste* (Northwest area travel guide) (Buenos Aires: Automóvil Club Argentino, 1944).

contribution because it is only relevant in its relation to the Spanish tradition.[20] The main purpose of Noel's interpretation is to indicate the influence of art movements from the Central Andes in order to promote the Argentine region's artistic value, an intervention that seems oriented to rescue colonial art from the indifference long shown it since the late-nineteenth-century historiography in Argentina.[21] Nonetheless, Noel does not avoid that interpretative legacy, and after mentioning the distinctive features of a Colla architectural current (with a lateral square tower) and a Calchaquí one (with two towers), he refers to "an extremely poor colonial scenery, which far from participating in the development of traditional forms further contributed to dissipate them as a result of the late Viceroyalty of the Río de la Plata establishment."[22]

The need to relate the nature of these buildings to "the face of the nation" is fully expressed in a foldable map included in issues three and four of the collection, which identifies some churches located between Jujuy and Salta provinces (fig. 12).[23] Noel draws a route with two main paths, and at certain points, he includes illustrations of churches surrounded by terrain and connected to other side roads. This pictorial map highlights the exterior features of the selected churches—what Noel refers to as "plastic appearance"—and shapes an image linked to his own desire to capture the connection between architecture and territory.[24] At the same time, this resource reaffirms the Indo-Hispanic legacy as an essential element of Argentina's artistic development, a conviction closely related to Noel's ideology in terms of cultural mestizaje, which connected the South Andean Indigenous persistence with the peninsular tradition imposed by the Spanish Conquest.

As the creator and disseminator of this thematic map, Noel proposes a very particular analysis of the region. The reference to different provinces with indefinite borders and the proximity of buildings promotes the image of a place filled with monuments and encompasses an idealization of the northwest as a social and cultural space. The map, which corresponds to Noel's own personal vision, includes the academy's stamp in the lower corner as a sign of authority and as an endorsement of the resource. Here, we see a prominent figure defining, under the protection of an official institution, what is valuable and worthy to be considered Argentine heritage.

Some of the churches and chapels selected by Noel (not part of a thorough registry, but

Fig. 15. "Grafico de las trayectorias historico-artisticas por el camino de los Incas y la Quebrada de Humahuaca," map by Martín Noel included in *Guía de viaje: zona noroeste* (Northwest area travel guide) (Buenos Aires: Automóvil Club Argentino, 1944), n.p.

Fig. 16. Colonial archaeological circles according to Pedro J. Vignale's sketch, map made by Martín Noel, in *Documentos de Arte Colonial Sudamericano: rutas históricas de la arquitectura virreinal altoperuana*, vol. 5 (Buenos Aires: Academia Nacional de Bellas Artes, 1948), n.p. Academia Nacional de Bellas Artes.

rather what Noel knew and chose for his map) were declared National Historic Monuments during those years, and restoration work began on a number of them. After the first appearance of Noel's map, we find other maps presented in the fourth National Salon of Architecture in 1943 that include monuments already designated as historical and prospective ones and also some town maps that incorporate the buildings' facades (fig. 13). In the context of these visual resources aimed at locating monuments and historical sites, we find again, some years later, Noel's northern map, along with the travel guides that the Automóvil Club Argentino (Argentine Automobile Club) began to publish in 1942 (figs. 14 and 15). The map in figure 15 illustrates one of the cultural articles that used to come with information for travelers, such as route maps. The way this map was distributed outside of the *Documentos de Arte Argentino*—in a reduced size and without its original purpose to serve as a graphic within a collection of documents—shows the impact this sort of image had outside of the academy. In addition, the supposed neutral and scientific nature of the cartographic record shows how this map effectively described a well-connected cultural region: a region connected by cultural routes that linked landscapes and monuments.[25]

Another parallel editorial project, *Documentos de Arte Colonial Sudamericano,* whose initial phase lasted from 1943 to 1951, also incorporated maps into its issues. Contrary to the *Documentos de Arte Argentino,* these issues focused on Bolivia, and later Peru, and were the result of a diplomatic exchange between the academy and the Ministry of Education and Indigenous Affairs from the neighboring country.[26] Included in issue five of that collection, titled "Historic routes of colonial architecture from the Upper Peru," is a foldable map, larger than the one I previously mentioned (see fig. 12), titled "Colonial archaeological circles according to Pedro J. Vignale's sketch" (fig. 16). Vignale had worked on the buildings' photographic record for the academy, and Noel was in charge of portraying that record by including pictures inside the map. Despite the difference in size between the northern Argentine and Bolivian maps, they share a common interest: to stress how routes and connections led to the development of a

Fig. 17. Outhouses adjacent to the church of Yavi, photograph by Hans Mann. *Documentos de Arte Argentino: La Iglesia de Yavi*, vol. 1 (Buenos Aires: Academia Nacional de Bellas Artes, 1939), 1. Academia Nacional de Bellas Artes.

Fig. 18. Hut and adobe walls, boundaries of the church, photograph by Hans Mann. *Documentos de Arte Argentino: La Iglesia de Yavi*, vol. 1 (Buenos Aires: Academia Nacional de Bellas Artes, 1939), 4. Academia Nacional de Bellas Artes.

regional architecture and to demonstrate the structural coincidences between the churches situated in each location. This matter is particularly emphasized by Noel in the introduction of that issue, when he writes: "Here we display an unrevealed collection of monuments, which, to add to their own merits, connect the artistic journey of the most important cities of the Upper Peru with northern Argentina."[27]

Going back to the *Documentos de Arte Argentino*, we find that the distribution of images inside the volumes leads us to think of a certain journey that avoids presenting each

Fig. 19. Cover of *Automovilismo* 23, no. 269 (May–June 1942).

monument in a direct manner—as was the case in the first issue dedicated to the church of Yavi. The series of consecutive images gradually introduces the church with its surrounding area, the residents, the buildings, and then the inside of the church and the art pieces. Different groups of images, thus, prevail. On the one hand, the staging, with people performing a subordinate role, acts as a frame of reference to the building in terms of scale or being part of the landscape's general view (figs. 17 and 18). These representations were deeply rooted in the folkloric vision encouraged by Noel in his essays. For instance, when referring to "somnambulant lives that wander through the immutable aridity of the altiplano," he describes the Indigenous communities frozen in time. In a similar way, the representations were also promoted through tourism since national monuments became popular during those years and proved to be an attraction for travelers (fig. 19).[28] In this regard, the series of photographic plates in *Documentos de Arte Argentino* was similar to the approach adopted by the maps in the sense that they downplayed the local communities and their role as involved in and protagonists of these buildings' social lives.

Even though this work in many ways is devoid of the local inhabitants, it provides a detailed registry of an almost unknown photographic collection. It documents the existence and state of the preservation of buildings and artistic objects that had not been predominant in previous editorial projects. Because colonial art from the Viceroyalty of Río de la Plata was dismissed as less important than art from other viceroyalties, this material was included, for the first time, as part of the nation's art history, introducing an innovative collection. Furthermore, many pictures taken by Mann were reutilized by the academy in

Fig. 20. Hans Mann's Archive, Academia Nacional de Bellas Artes.

their following publications during the 1970s and 1980s, which shows the importance this photographic archive (fig. 20).

Conclusion

This editorial agenda carried out by the academy is traditionally associated with a preprofessional phase of art historical writing and with the way that vernacular architecture was understood from a Western architectural point of view.[29] However, even beyond the brief examples given above, the academy adopted a rhetoric concerning the production of its graphic resources that revealed the power that the organization had to select and classify images from the past. In that sense, *Documentos de Arte Argentino* doesn't belong to the preprofessional stage but instead, it singularly highlighted a collection hardly considered in previous studies and prioritized a combination of essayistic writing and illustrations rather than a text with a critical approach. Additionally, in order to better understand the place the academy held within official institutions at the time, it is important to analyze the role this collection played in the recognition of a national heritage, which also promoted broader interests. In other words: the addition of the artistic production from the viceregal period to an official Argentine art history became a reference point not only for the academy to establish its own importance but also to promote this work's valorization beyond its own space.

Martín Noel played a pioneering and crucial role in establishing Argentine colonial art as an object of study, and his position within the academy allowed him to connect official fine arts with the broader interest in a Hispanic American artistic legacy. As early as 1914, he held a conference in the rooms of the Museo Nacional de Bellas Artes de Buenos Aires (National Museum of Fine Arts) and exhibited, for the first time, a slide show with pictures of Bolivian and Peruvian architecture.[30] Noel obtained these images during his initial journey through South America. A few years later, he published an article about it in the University of Buenos Aires' magazine, *Revista de Arquitectura*.[31] Noel's project happened within the still-young institution—the Museo Nacional de Bellas Artes was only founded in 1896—whose mission was to collect "universal art" in order to "develop" local artistic taste.[32] Noel's intellectual project was slightly different than the academy's, so it was doubly significant during these early years that it placed an emphasis on a set of regional places, objects, and images that were not part of the current artistic debates. Despite the geographical limitations of his approach and the stress put on certain examples from the continent, his project began to reaffirm the horizon of interpretation for the study of Latin American art in Argentina—the Viceroyalty of Peru as the principal focus for artistic production. Historically, art and architecture in the Río de la Plata territory was not as deserving as that from other viceroyalties, and so to incorporate Argentine art into the Latin American sphere, Noel adopted a regional perspective that recovered the south-central Andean tradition as a precedent for Argentina's own artistic production.[33]

While the 1914 conference represented a landmark in Noel's career and postulated the relevance of documentary images in the development of art history, *Documentos de Arte Argentino* was a crucial part of the recognition and systematic dissemination of local heritage. Noel's intellectual project spurred the implementation of cultural policies, which allowed the distribution of cultural material to reach new areas and fostered a national architecture that people could visit, pass through, and take pictures of. It is in the early issues devoted to the northwest where we see Noel's achievements, which are then emulated in the rest of the collection as a key historiographic element.

Notes

1. Martín Noel, quoted in Margarita Gutman, "El Pabellón Argentino en la Exposición Iberoamericana de Sevilla," in *El arquitecto Martín Noel: Su tiempo y su obra*, ed. Ramón Gutiérrez et al. (Seville, Spain: Junta de Andalucía, 1995), 154.

2. José Luis Romero, *Las ideas en la Argentina del siglo XX*, rev. ed. (1965; repr., Buenos Aires: Biblioteca Actual, 1987), 55.

3. Ricardo Rojas, *Eurindia: Ensayo de estética fundado en la experiencia histórica de las culturas americanas* (Buenos Aires: Librería La Facultad, 1924).

4. Alejandro Cattaruzza, *Los usos del pasado: La historia y la política argentinas en discusión, 1910-1945* (Buenos Aires: Editorial Sudamericana, 2007).

5. *II° Congreso internacional de historia de América*, vol. 1 (Buenos Aires: Academia Nacional de la Historia, 1938), 407.

6. Acta n. 34 (November 22, 1938) in *Actas*, vol. 1, 123.

7. Mariana Giordano and Patricia Méndez, "La fotografía de Hans Mann, pionera en el patrimonio cultural," in *Hans Mann: Miradas sobre el patrimonio cultural*, eds. Ramón Gutiérrez and Patricia Méndez (Buenos Aires: CEDODAL - Academia Nacional de Bellas Artes, 2004), 11-20.

8. Martín Noel's speech in "Cámara de Diputados: Comisión de Museos," in *Boletín de la Comisión Nacional de Museos y de Monumentos y Lugares Históricos* 3, no. 3 (1941): 251.

9. Acta n. 34, 123.

10. Anahí Ballent's studies about tourism and cultural heritage led me to think about the possibility of this relationship. See in particular Anahí Ballent, "Monumentos, turismo e historia: imágenes del noroeste en la arquitectura promovida por el estado, 1935-45," *Jornadas Perspectivas Históricas sobre el Estado Argentino*, 2003, unpublished.

11. Ibid.

12. Melina Piglia, *Autos, rutas y turismo: El Automóvil Club Argentino y el Estado* (Buenos Aires: Siglo Veintiuno Editores, 2014), 188.

13. Anahí Ballent, "Kilómetro cero: la construcción del universo simbólico del camino en la Argentina de los años 30," *Boletín del Instituto de Historia Argentina y Americana Dr. Emilio Ravignani* 3, no. 27 (2005): 117.

14. About the conditions in which the National Roads Law was created, see Piglia, *Autos, rutas y turismo*, part II.

15. Acta n. 43 (September 12, 1939) in *Actas*, vol. 1, 153.

16. Martín Noel, "La Iglesia de Yavi," in *Documentos de Arte Argentino: La Iglesia de Yavi*, vol. 1 (Buenos Aires: Academia Nacional de Bellas Artes, 1939), 8.

17. Jorge Tomasi, "Mirando lo vernáculo: tradiciones disciplinares en el estudio de las "otras arquitecturas' en la Argentina del siglo XX," *AREA*, no. 17 (October 2011): 73.

18. Noel, "La Iglesia de Yavi," 10.

19. Ibid., 11.

20. Ballent, "Monumentos, turismo e historia."

21. Particularly, in early Eduardo Schiaffino's texts about Argentine art. See Eduardo Schiaffino, *La evolución del gusto artístico en Buenos Aires*, ed. Godofredo E. J. Canale (Buenos Aires: F. A. Colombo, 1982).

22. Noel, "La Iglesia de Yavi," 9.

23. Noel's speech in "Cámara de Diputados: Comisión de Museos," 252.

24. Ibid., 251.

25. Regarding the maps and the debate about their scientific value and the representational status, I return to the theoretical balance proposed by Carla Lois in *Mapas para la nación: episodios en la historia de la cartografía Argentina* (Buenos Aires: Editorial Biblos, 2014).

26. Acta no. 79 (October 9, 1942) in *Actas*, vol. 1, 297–99.

27. Martín Noel, "Rutas históricas de la arquitectura colonial altoperuana," in *Documentos de Arte Colonial Sudamericano: Rutas históricas de la arquitectura colonial altoperuana*, vol. 5 (Buenos Aires: Academia Nacional de Bellas Artes, 1948), viii.

28. Martín Noel, *Palabras en acción. Apologías y temas de historia, arte y urbanismo* (Buenos Aires: Peuser, 1945), 254.

29. See Carla Guillermina García, *Historia del arte y universidad: la experiencia del Instituto de Arte Americano e Investigaciones Estéticas y la consolidación disciplinar de la historiografía artística en la Argentina (1946-1970)* (Buenos Aires: Instituto de Arte Americano e Investigaciones Estéticas, 2020); Tomasi, "Mirando lo vernáculo," 73.

30. "La arquitectura colonial," *La Nación*, September 22, 1914, 7.

31. Martín Noel, "Comentarios sobre el nacimiento de la arquitectura hispano-Americana," *Revista de Arquitectura*, no. 1 (1915): 8–12.

32. Laura Malosetti Costa, *Los primeros modernos: arte y sociedad en Buenos Aires a fines del siglo XIX* (Buenos Aires: Fondo de Cultura Económica, 2001).

33. See Laura Malosetti Costa, Gabriela Siracusano, and Ana María Telesca, "Impacto de la 'moderna' historiografía europea en la construcción de los primeros relatos de la historia del arte argentino," in *In(disciplinas): estética e historia del arte en el cruce de los discursos: XXII Coloquio Internacional de Historia del Arte* (Mexico City: Universidad Nacional Autónoma de México, Instituto de Investigaciones Estéticas, 1999), 395–425.

ANA ELENA MALLET

Neocolonial Design in Mexico, 1940–1970: From a Lost Heritage to a Modern Vocabulary

At the end of the Mexican Revolution, the new regime designed a strategy to pacify the country: a project associated with national identity to standardize a territory with a great diversity of cultures. This national project, rooted in a heroic idea of the Indigenous past, would also generate a series of reflections on the architectural style in which the country should be rebuilt in the wake of this civil conflict.

In this context, the Architecture Talks, which took place in 1933, two decades after the revolution, are consequential. They involved heated discussions between contemporary architects, who sought to define the national style and whose discourse permeated into the design of furniture and everyday objects. That October, the Society of Mexican Architects (SAM) organized a series of conversations at the library of the Academy of San Carlos on modern architecture and the paths it had taken, as well as on the craft and labor of the architect. Participating architects established their positions, and it was perhaps these dialogues that, to a large extent, determined the path that modern architecture would follow in Mexico.

An academic categorization of Mexican architects emerged from this debate: the "Integrists," who, as their name suggests, were willing to *integrate* styles from other historical moments; the "Radicals," who sought to purge architecture of all ornamentation and understand it as a tool for generating solutions; and the "Socialists," whose goal was to bring the postulates of urban Functionalism to the countryside.[1]

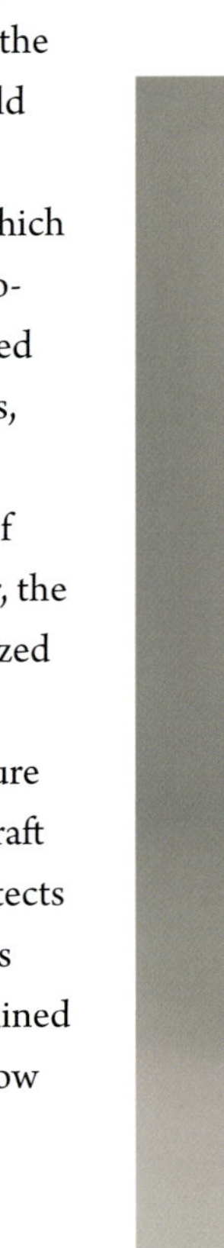

Fig. 1. Unknown artist, *Butaque* Armchair, 1780–1820. Spanish cedar, leather, and metal, 36¼ × 27½ × 28¾ in. (92.1 × 69.9 × 73 cm). Denver Art Museum: Funds from the Carl Patterson bequest, 2021.99.

The debate on the functional versus the beautiful, on the one hand, and the simple and the clean versus the highly ornamental, on the other, was also translated into the world of design. While these aspects were not explicitly discussed by designers at the time, they were nevertheless reflected in the pieces they created, which sought to respond to different markets and tastes. There were those who still preferred to design furniture and accessories associated with historical styles like Chippendale, Louis XV, Queen Anne, and the like, those who fought to create new styles associated with Mexico's tradition and/or past, and those who looked to the European avant-garde and sought to imitate its products. For a good part of the Mexican elite, good taste and class were associated with old European styles.

All of the artistic disciplines of that time—painting, sculpture, literature, design, and architecture—were immersed in this debate. Nevertheless, all of these currents continued to coexist without cancelling each other out. At the same time that Luis Barragán (1902–1988) was developing his architectural project rooted in regional values, Mario Pani (1911–1993) took up the principles of Le Corbusier (1887–1965) and built the first residential complex in Latin America based on the aesthetic of the Swiss architect.[2] Likewise, while Diego Rivera (1886–1957), as the most prominent representative of nationalism in Mexican painting, executed murals and easel paintings with Indigenous and patriotic themes, Germán Cueto (1893–1975), continuing the precepts of the Estridentista movement in which he had been involved and influenced by modern art and the European avant-garde, created pieces that distanced themselves from those themes.[3]

In questions of design, Clara Porset (1895–1981) chose to reconceptualize Mexican folk furniture to make it more ergonomic and sophisticated. In a parallel fashion, Camilo López's (1896–1979) Galerías Chippendale sold reproductions of historical styles. The writer Jorge Cuesta and the Contemporáneos group, who were inclined toward opening themselves to European influences in literature, issued continual diatribes in magazines and other print media against writers such as Ermilo Abreu Gómez and Héctor Pérez Jiménez, who favored a nationalist literature focused on purely Mexican themes. This debate was captured in the 1932 pamphlet by Alfonso Reyes titled *A vuelta de correo*, which reflected on cosmopolitan principles and called for peace between both factions, proclaiming that the town was big enough for the both of them.[4]

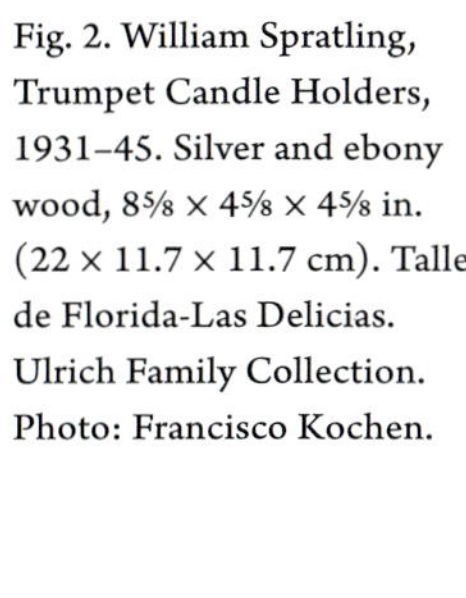

Fig. 2. William Spratling, Trumpet Candle Holders, 1931–45. Silver and ebony wood, 8⅝ × 4⅝ × 4⅝ in. (22 × 11.7 × 11.7 cm). Taller de Florida-Las Delicias. Ulrich Family Collection. Photo: Francisco Kochen.

Between the 1930s and '50s, there was an intermittent debate between the domestic and the foreign (or the Europeanizing), a battle that no one really won. What can be said is that these two currents have coexisted up until the present day: one that believes that an authentic identity can be found in turning to one's roots and traditions and another that looks abroad to develop a language of one's own.

In this essay, I look at distinct manifestations of the Neocolonial in different time periods. In places like Taxco in Guerrero, the San Angel neighborhood in Mexico City, or Marfil in Guanajuato, I explore different expressions of the style and its social reception. I also consider design objects like the *butaque*, a vernacular mestizo chair type that is the result of the fusion of two cultures: Indigenous and Spanish (fig. 1). Reviewing these different examples will allow the reader to understand the plurality of the Neocolonial style in Mexican design across many decades.

New Repertoires Based on the Colonial Past

The recuperation of Spanish aesthetics, associated with an elegant, distinctive colonial past, also formed part of these discussions about national identity, even before the postrevolutionary period. The 1901 book by the US historian Sylvester Baxter, *Spanish-Colonial Architecture in Mexico*, shows a marked interest in this theme.[5] Likewise, in 1904, Porfirio Díaz commissioned the German photographer Guillermo Kahlo (1872–1941) to photograph religious architecture, which resulted in a 1909 album, limited to twenty copies that were distributed among government officials. It was not until after the revolution, in 1924, that the painter Gerardo Murillo (1875–1964), known as Dr. Atl, compiled these images and made them public in the book *Iglesias de México*.[6]

Around the same time, the Youth Atheneum, founded in 1909, hosted debates on the construction of a national identity that would acknowledge revolutionary values and the viceregal past in order to erase the French influence that had so captivated the dictator Porfirio Díaz; these debates found an echo in the discourse of the architect Federico Mariscal (1881–1971). Mariscal, who had a master's degree in architecture from the Academy of San Carlos, was a proponent of studying and restoring colonial buildings that remained standing, many of which were threatened. In his series of lectures at the Popular Mexican University in 1913–14, which were later collected into a single volume, the architect argued that "Mexican architecture should be that which emerged and developed during the three centuries of the Viceroyalty, in which Mexicanness was constituted."[7]

Fig. 3. William Spratling, Armchair, ca. 1940. Wood and leather, 29⅞ × 21¼ × 18½ in. (76 × 54 × 47 cm). Consuelo + Violante Ulrich Collection. Photo: Jorge Vertiz.

It was in the midst of these debates that the US designer and architect William Spratling (1900–1967) came to Mexico in 1929, setting up in Taxco to open a silver workshop, followed by a furniture workshop, then a tin, and finally a textiles workshop (fig. 2). During his first decade of production, Spratling organized a system that would train artisans in silversmithing until they became professionals that could establish themselves as independent agents. This allowed for the creation of an informal Taxco school of silverwork, whose distinctive style prevailed until well into the 1980s. That early stage was characterized by a series of aesthetic explorations in order to define a style. In an article published in 1968, the designer himself stated that "a style cannot be created from one day to the next. I must confess that, since the days of 1931, my style had a long road to travel in Mexican metalwork."[8]

Spratling found inspiration in references to Indigenous and folk art and to rural life and its elements, but he also explored neocolonial vocabularies. The designer could thus offer all that was considered to be "Mexican" in those years in his store. His aesthetic explorations sparked a type of regional aesthetic, and his products became objects of desire. As Daniel Rubín de la Borbolla said at the time, "[Spratling] redesigned and began to manufacture furniture of a regional rural type, which quickly became popular."[9]

Since Taxco is a city with predominantly colonial architecture, it would seem self-evident to reference these styles and produce a furniture series that spoke to preexisting buildings and their imagery. Spratling produced reinterpretations of Spanish friar's chairs and antique butaques, high tables with carved legs, low tables covered in cowhide with wrought iron studs, drying racks, and dressers with colonial-style moldings, among many other pieces (figs. 3 and 4).

Fig. 4. William Spratling, Baby Chair, ca. 1940. Wood and leather, 28⅞ × 14⅝ × 12⅜ in. (73.5 × 37 × 31.5 cm). Consuelo + Violante Ulrich Collection. Photo: Jorge Vertiz.

To a large extent, driven by Spratling's growing popularity, Taxco became a cultural hotbed between the 1930s and '50s, an obligatory stop for domestic and international tourists traveling to Acapulco, who took the opportunity to acquire products with the Spratling seal. In the 1950s, Spratling pieces became so highly sought after that other workshops began to reproduce and reinterpret these pieces, in what became known as the "Colonial Taxco" style.[10] Even Hollywood star Marilyn Monroe traveled to Mexico in February 1962, a few months before her death. Besides drinking tequila with the filmmaker Emilio "El Indio" Fernández and his wife, the actress Columba Domínguez, and eating at the famed taqueria El Taquito in downtown Mexico City, Monroe traveled to

Taxco and purchased a large set of furniture and design objects from Spratling and other Taxco artisans to furnish her newly acquired neocolonial mansion in Brentwood, California.

The relationship between the Mexican Neocolonial and the Mission Revival styles in California is a fascinating architectural link that reflects the cultural interconnection and historical influence between the two regions. In the late nineteenth and early twentieth centuries, both architectural styles emerged in a context that sought to define a unique cultural identity and express a sense of nostalgia. Inspired by the colonial architectural forms of Mexico's viceregal era, the Neocolonial style sought to recover and reinterpret prehispanic and colonial architectural elements, creating an aesthetic that fused Indigenous and Spanish traditions. Elements such as arches, interior patios, and tile details characterized this style, symbolizing Mexico's national identity during the postrevolutionary period. Meanwhile, Mission Revival developed in the late nineteenth century in California as part of the Arts and Crafts movement and the Panama-California Exposition held in San Diego in 1915. Inspired by the Spanish missions established in California during the eighteenth century, architects adopted elements such as arcades, bell towers, tile roofs, and adobe details to evoke the appearance of the original missions. Unlike Mexican Neocolonial style, Mission Revival focused on the Franciscan missions in California, fusing Spanish Colonial architecture with Native American elements. The reinterpretation of Mexican Neocolonial style in California fused with the Mission Revival aesthetic and reflected the search for a common regional identity.

The popularity of both styles coincided with a resurgence of interest in historical and cultural heritage, as well as a boom in tourism in the region. By combining colonial elements with a modern aesthetic, these architectural styles helped define California's distinctive architectural image and solidified its connection to Mexico's rich history. Mexican Neocolonial style and the Mission Revival in California are visual testaments to a shared history and the evolution of cultural identity in these regions.

Fig. 5. Felix Tissot, Tureens from the *Colonial White* line, ca. 1970. Earthenware, small tureen: 2¾ × 6¾ × 4⅛ in. dia. (70 × 17.1 × 10.5 cm), lid: 3½ in. dia. (8.9 cm); medium tureen: 4 × 9 × 5¾ in. dia. (10.2 × 22.9 × 14.6 cm), lid: 2¾ × 6¼ in. dia. (7 × 15.9 cm), signed "Felix Tissot Taxco"; large tureen: 7½ × 11¼ × 7½ in. dia. (19.1 × 28.6 × 19.1 cm), lid: 3⅜ × 7½ in. (8.5 × 19.1 cm), signed "Felix Tissot Taxco." Place of production: Taxco, Guerrero. Ione Tissot Collection, Guerrero. Photo: Francisco Kochen.

Spratling was aware of this shared heritage and knew how to promote it with wealthy and famous clients and friends who visited Taxco. His well-earned fame in the United States and a certain commercial presence specifically in California at Gump's store, which sold his silverware, contributed to his successful operation.

The Neocolonial style of Taxco created by Spratling influenced other workshops and creators: the fashion designer Tachi Castillo (1918–1999), sister of the renowned silversmiths Antonio, Chato, and Coco Castillo—who had trained under Spratling—consolidated her fashion house through the reinterpretation and romanticization of typically peasant garments associated with the Spanish missions in California and popularized through Hollywood films such as *Ramona* (1928), starring Dolores del Río, which fed the neocolonial imaginary of Taxco. The white cotton Bertha blouse, with a round neckline with profuse frills and a clear colonial and rural inspiration, was one of Castillo's signature pieces that was sold in boutiques across the southern United States and in Mexico City at her store in Zona Rosa and at her stand in Bazaar Sábado.

The French ceramicist Felix Tissot (1909–1989) came to Taxco in 1953 to open a workshop that would popularize colorful designs resembling Indigenous ones found in amate paper, in collaboration with artisans from Ameyaltepec and Xalitla in Guerrero state. In the 1970s, aware that Neocolonial styles were back in vogue, particularly among the Mexican bourgeoisie and political class (a matter to which I will return), he launched his *Colonial White* line of plates, bowls, and full dinnerware sets in pristine white (figs. 5–7), with reliefs and finishes that were directly inspired by original colonial ceramics or the Chinese export ceramic designed specifically for the New Spain market (figs. 8 and 9).

The designer Antonio Frausto Martínez (1926–2020) was perhaps the last to explore the neocolonial vocabulary in Taxco furniture in the 1960s and became a promoter of this style in the second half of the twentieth century. Having grown up in Mexico City, he returned to his hometown of Taxco in 1956 in order to open a store named Xila, where he sold his neocolonial designs. His furniture was made from heavy hardwoods that, when hand-carved, resulted in elegant, curved lines and geometric patterns that provided aesthetic balance. Embossed details, such as arabesques and scrolls, lent a distinctive decorative character. The hardware used, such as handles and hinges in flat black iron, were elaborately designed to complement the overall visual language of the furniture. The color palette tended to be warm and earthy, with rich wood tones that highlighted the natural beauty of the material. In addition, the application of finishes that enhanced the texture of the carved wood, providing luster and protection, was common.

In a few short years, he became popular with tourists and local visitors alike and opened a second furniture store in the posh Zona Rosa neighborhood in Mexico City. His collaborations with the architects Francisco Artigas (1916–1999) and Carlos Obregón Formoso (1905–1981) in the interior design of their domestic spaces were fundamental in placing him in the spotlight and repositioning the Neocolonial style in the taste and imaginary of the Mexican elites.

The Butaque: From America to Europe and Back

Spratling was also one of the first Mexico-based designers to revise and reinterpret the typology of the butaque, a vernacular piece that predates

Right: Fig. 6. Felix Tissot, Platter from the *Colonial White* line, ca. 1970. Earthenware, ⅜ × 17¾ × 11⅞ in. (1 × 45.1 × 30.2 cm), signed "Felix Tissot Taxco México." Place of production: Taxco, Guerrero. Ione Tissot Collection, Taxco, Guerrero. Photo: Francisco Kochen.

Far right: Fig. 7. Felix Tissot, Plate from the *Colonial White* line, ca. 1970. Earthenware, ⅜ × 10½ in. dia. (1 × 26.7 cm dia.), signed "Felix Tissot Taxco." Place of production: Taxco, Guerrero. Ione Tissot Collection, Taxco, Guerrero. Photo: Francisco Kochen.

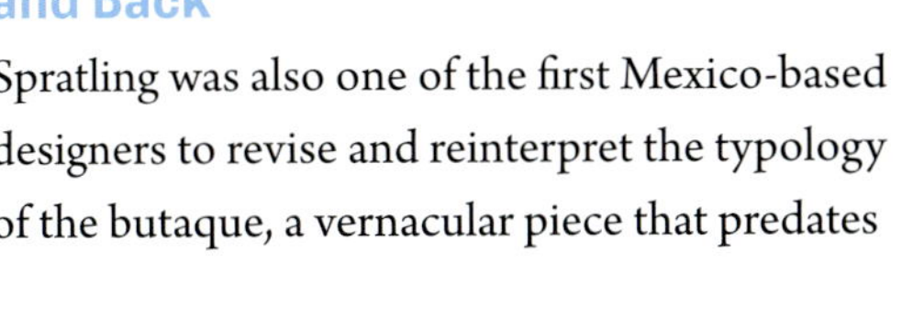

the encounter between the Spanish and the Mexica, whose history and genealogy in Latin America has been painstakingly studied by Jorge Rivas Pérez.

Rivas Pérez situates the origins of this hybrid piece, which arose from the intersection of history, tradition, and cultural exchange, in Cumaná, Venezuela, at the end of the sixteenth century. It combines elements from two different chairs: the low, curved, inclined form emerged from the wooden *dúho*, while its legs and the construction process using wooden joints were made possible thanks to the technology and design of the Spanish Savonarola chair.[11] In New Spain, the first mention of the butaque goes back to the cargo manifestos of ships sailing from Campeche to Veracruz, as Campeche was one of the centers for the production and export of this chair.[12] The butaque was rapidly disseminated throughout Mexico. As this piece of furniture became an essential part of the country's mestizo heritage, it developed anonymous, community-based regional variations, rather than an authorial design.

Spratling made several versions of the butaque (fig. 10). Some were lower and wider, and some had a fretwork heart design on the upper part of the back. The most popular model was a little higher, with armrests in the form of a comma and a cowhide seat with thick wrought iron studs. The back was crowned by two lateral posts and, in the center, a fretwork fish design that became emblematic of Spratling's work that he used to sign some of his pieces with a hot iron brand.

Other Mexico-based designers, such as Michael van Beuren (1911–2004) with the Miguelito and San Miguelito or Don Shoemaker (1920–1990) with the Sloucher chair, created iterations of the butaque, integrating it into their commercial production lines (figs. 11 and 12). But it was the Cuban Mexican designer Clara Porset who would make the butaque into her signature piece and a fundamental element of her search for a design style of her own, one that would represent a modern discourse while still associated with a place, a national heritage, and a vernacular tradition (fig. 13).

In 1948, Porset published the article "Folk Furniture of Mexico" in the monographic issue on Mexico of the academic journal *School Arts*, a publication dedicated to issues associated with

Fig. 8. Platter commemorating the coronation of Charles IV with the coat of arms of Mexico City, 1700s, China. Porcelain with polychrome glaze and gold varnish, 18½ × 11¾ in. (47 × 30 cm). Franz Mayer Museum Collection, Mexico City. Photo: Francisco Kochen.

Fig. 9. Plate, 1700s, China. Porcelain with polychrome glaze and gold varnish, 9⅞ in. dia. (25 cm dia.). Franz Mayer Museum Collection, Mexico City. Photo: Francisco Kochen.

Above: Fig. 10. William Spratling, *Heart*, ca. 1940. Wood and cowhide, 31¼ × 20½ × 19½ in. (79.5 × 52 × 49.5 cm). Consuelo + Violante Ulrich Collection. Photo: Jorge Vertiz.

arts education, in which she studied and analyzed a large number of pieces of traditional Mexican furniture, with an explanation of their uses, forms, and materials.[13] Porset argued that vernacular Mexican furniture, chairs in particular, are mestizo pieces: the product of the fusion of the cultures of prehispanic Mexico and Spain. She also argued that denying this hybrid origin would be to turn one's back on history, and she reflected on how these pieces are now so integrated into the landscape that they are considered to be vernacular, belonging to a particular locality, with each community giving it unique characteristics. Porset recounted how some of these typologies came from the old continent and took on new characteristics as they took root

Right: Fig. 11. Michael van Beuren, *San Miguelito*, ca. 1947. Primavera wood and cotton fabric, 29⅞ × 28¾ × 25⅝ in. (76 × 73 × 65 cm). Jan van Beuren Collection. Photo: Jorge Vertiz.

in Mexican—and even American—territory and began to be built with local materials.

Besides educating readers on its cultural values, Porset managed to understand the butaque's structural characteristics and how it took advantage of its materials, using small planks of wood to achieve the curvature of its legs, seat and back, which generated very little waste and ensured very secure joints, thanks to the large degree of surface contact between each piece. Porset realized that the continual curve between the seat and the back is a central element of the design; if executed poorly, it interfered with the chair's comfort and ease of use. She experimented with variations in the dimensions of the structure and the materials used in the chair, trying out a large variety of different fabrics. Over the years, she concentrated on a process that involved an ergonomic analysis of the butaque's structure in order to modify it, thus achieving different proportions and finishes.

A Neocolonial Style from San Ángel to Guanajuato

The Neocolonial has been one of the most prolific and enduring styles in the history of Mexican design. Its association with prosperous times and its class and distinction mean the style becomes popular every so often, and new reinterpretations emerge. Architect Manuel Parra (1911–1997) was a leader in one of the reinterpretations. Some critics have named him the precursor to that "other Mexican architecture" that, in a sense, denied the modernism associated with Functionalism and the International Style.

Parra, who had a long career, began intermittently working in Guanajuato in the 1960s. Previously, in Mexico City, he had distinguished himself by using a constructivist style based on neocolonial typology in the neighboring towns of San Ángel and part of Coyoacán. The house of filmmaker Emilio "El Indio" Fernández, which he began to build in 1946 and remodeled several times up until 1965, became a neocolonial landmark, charting the path for Parra's architectural language, which was characterized by the recycling of building materials from demolished colonial-era structures. His distinctive style countered the popular modernist styles associated with Europe that impacted conceptions of modern Mexican architecture in those years and didn't easily coordinate with existing commercial furniture. As a result, Parra decided to design much of the furniture that accompanied his spaces.

Fig. 12. Don Shoemaker, *Sling* Chair, *Sloucher* line, ca. 1960. Cocolobo wood and leather, 27⅛ × 22⅞ × 28 in. (69 × 58 × 71 cm). Señal S.A., Santa María de Guido, Michoacán. Alonso de Garay Collection. Photo: Jorge Vertiz.

Fig. 13. Clara Porset for Casa Gálvez, *Butaque* Chair, design ca. 1940, edition 1955–56. Bald-cypress wood and woven crane, 28¾ × 22⅞ × 23¼ in. (73 × 58 × 59 cm). Gálvez Guzzy Family Collection. Photo: Guillermo Soto.

Perhaps the architect's most recurring piece was his butaque, but his repertoire also included other colonial typologies, such as ladder-back chairs, ladies' chairs or rush chairs, scissor chairs, and friar's chairs. He also designed tables, cabinets, and enormous dressers, following his architectural principles: recovering material from original colonial objects and constructions in order to reposition—and resignify—it as part of a new piece of furniture. Parra's objects and buildings mixed old and new, reused and new materials, in order to give his pieces a sense of timelessness.

Between 1945 and 1965, Parra designed and furnished over forty houses in the San Ángel district. The houses had original, colonial wooden beams mixed with modern ceramic tiles in the floors and ceilings. In the 1960s, he split his time between Mexico City and Guanajuato, where he continued designing furniture and restored and remodeled historic buildings, turning them into artists' workshops and residences. He was also involved in public housing projects that put forward new residential models for the working class.

It was also in Guanajuato, in the old mining zone of Marfil, a colonial enclave from 1550s, that the Italian architect and designer Giorgio Belloli (1907–1971) led a furniture design initiative associated with the Neocolonial style. Originally based in Tucson, Arizona, he came to the old mining town in 1953, attracted by the state's colonial past. He ended up staying thanks to local politicians who sought to revitalize Marfil's colonial heritage and architecture after years of neglect and promised tax-free land for

Fig. 14. Giorgio Belloli's house in Marfil, Guanajuato. Photograph from Verna Cook Shipway, *Mexican Interiors* (New York: Architectural Book Publishing Co., 1964), 13.

Fig. 15. Giorgio Belloli's house in Marfil, Guanajuato. Photograph from Verna Cook Shipway, *Mexican Interiors* (New York: Architectural Book Publishing Co., 1964), 12.

Fig. 16. Alejandro Rangel Hidalgo, *Butaque Rangelino*, undated. Mahogany wood and cowhide, 24¾ × 31½ × 36⅝ in. (63 × 80 × 93 cm). Collection of de la Madrid Cordero. Photo: Jorge Vertiz.

three years to anyone who was willing to restore old colonial buildings and take up permanent residence in the area.[14]

Belloli bought the Santa Ana and La Trinidad, seventeenth-century haciendas, and dedicated himself to restoring them, and then he subdivided the properties for sale. Belloli took advantage of an interesting migration route between Tucson and Guanajuato, where American clients bought the restored buildings and ordered furniture, metalwork, and other objects for their new homes. Belloli already had a history as an antique salesman and furniture designer in Tucson, where, like, Parra, he used materials and adornments from demolished colonial buildings to create new pieces. Belloli lived at Santa Ana for over a decade, designing objects for his home that were featured in the books by Verna and Warren Shipway that popularized Mexican culture in the US market (figs. 14 and 15).

During the 1950s, specialized journals, academic conferences, and real estate developments, such as Jardines de Pedregal, more often promoted Functionalism and the International Style. The furniture designs of Michael van Beuren, originally functionalist and later associated with the Danish styles that became fashionable on the international market, inundated local stores. During these years, few designers and architects opted for a neocolonial language; Parra's and Belloli's explorations of the Neocolonial in San Ángel, Coyoacán, and Marfil signaled a gesture of rebellion and resistance. Both architects, enamored with history, were fighting modernist progress and new styles. They were willing and

Fig. 17. Antonio Attolini Lack, Chair, 1990. Oyamel wood and cowhide, 31½ × 31½ × 31½ in. (80 × 80 × 80 cm). Antonio Attolini Lack Archive Collection. Photo: Jorge Vertiz.

convinced to keep San Ángel and Marfil as historical enclaves, for Mexican traditional elites, conserving original colonial styles and reinterpreting the colonial to preserve social stature and good taste.

Between 1960 and 1970, Verna Cook Shipway and her husband Warren Shipway published five books dedicated to "Mexicanness" in architecture, design, and decoration, which were very well received.[15] These books, written in English and aimed at a US public, were dedicated to promoting the idea of the ideal Mexican house with an enduring style, a construction based on various layers of history, combining Indigenous, colonial, and modern objects in a nostalgic environment. Colonial and neocolonial mansions, reconstructed haciendas, vacation homes that evoked missions, urban mansions in a neoclassical style, and certain examples of modern architecture all appeared in black-and-white. Their pages also showed restored colonial and neocolonial decorations, such as the ironwork, mosaics, patios, and fountains, as well as the largely artisanal antique and modern objects, with which residents coexisted. The image of Mexico promoted by the Shipways was in opposition to that displayed by local architectural magazines such as *Arquitectura México* and *Espacios*, which instead promoted European and American designs with a meticulous, restless modernity. While some academics have argued that the Shipways' project denied the modernity that Mexico was embracing at the time, it's more the case that they were putting forward a vision of another modernity: one rooted in tradition, history, and the colonial past, open to coexistence with artisanal objects whose regional languages had a national imprint.[16]

Fig. 18. Ricardo Legorreta in collaboration with Emilio Guerrero, *Vallarta*, 1971. Cedar wood, palm, and natural varnish, 29⅜ × 21¼ × 19½ in. (74.5 × 54 × 49 cm). Legorreta Collection. Photo: Jaime Navarro Soto.

By the early 1970s, with the arrival of President Luis Echeverría, new ways of celebrating Mexican culture and looking to the past were promoted, which generated a new sense of national pride. From the creation of the Fondo Nacional para el Fomento de las Artesanías (FONART) in order to motivate traditional, handmade products to receptions at the presidential house where guests had to wear typical Mexican costumes, this neo-Mexicanism presented new interpretations of the colonial. Neocolonial and historicist styles in furniture had once again become part of the tastes of the elite, who, with a renewed sense of pride and ancestry, made these pieces part of their identity and a mark of their cultural level and social status (fig. 16).

The Neocolonial styles of the first half of the twentieth century were associated with the search for—and definition of—a national

Fig. 19. Residence in San José Iturbide, restoration 1963. Roberto and Fernando Luna Archive. Courtesy of LIGA Espacio para arquitectura. Photo: Fernando Luna.

identity, as the historian Johanna Lozoya Meckes argues, through "an ornamental version of New Spanish forms (baroque and missionary), a representation of *criollo* values or an eclectic historicist architecture connected to José Vasconcelos's educational policies and the cultural discourse of the Mexican Atheneum."[17] The "colonial style" objects, or that eclectic style advertised as being "colonial" in the catalogs of brands and designers from the late 1950s to the 1970s, are connected to social and class pretensions, reflecting the desires of the Mexican middle and upper classes to declare themselves to be both cosmopolitan and ancestral, proud of their Hispanic roots and seeking to consolidate their social position by emphasizing their lineage and "good taste," which involved appealing to the "history" of a "European" character.

Felix Tissot's *Colonial White* dinnerware line and Antonio Frausto's furniture, like Don Shoemaker's Española and Colonial furniture collections, Francisco Artigas's neocolonial homes, and even Clara Porset's rereadings of the friar's chair for the Churubusco Golf Club in 1964 are all a response to the social pretensions of the time, in which the political class and the business elite proudly embraced their Spanish roots.

A Modern Regionalism: The Mexican Dream

The search for a Mexican style in architecture during the first half of the twentieth century encouraged Enrique del Moral (1906–1987) to incorporate rural and colonial elements into a regional architecture. Luis Barragán's style also incorporated the local rural elements but drew as much from Spanish architecture and its Moorish influence as it did from vernacular constructions in Jalisco.[18] The success of Barragán's formula and its dissemination overseas paved the way for other architects to consolidate a Mexican style in architecture and to explore furniture design that coordinated with their architectural style. Antonio Attolini Lack (1931–2012) and Ricardo Legorreta (1931–2011) have been considered by many specialists to be representative of an architectural regionalism, largely influenced by Barragán, the modern movement associated with the International Style, and the convent architecture and monumentality of New Spain.[19]

Both Attolini Lack and Legorreta took up the typology of colonial furniture (rush chairs, armchairs, friar's chairs, ladder-back chairs, and butaques), forms that had been considered to be "vernacular designs," "anonymous," and therefore part of the national tradition for decades. These architects designed objects, accessories, and furniture for their hotels and residences, thinking of the "total artwork" as well as the comfort and refinement of their clients and the spaces created for them.[20] Attolini Lack personally designed the furniture for his apartments, which were then produced in different artisanal workshops (fig. 17). The monumentality of his domestic spaces opened the door for grandiloquent designs with honest materials associated with the local and national traditions, which had already incorporated the colonial.

In 1968, Legorreta designed the Hotel Camino Real in Mexico City—built for the nineteenth Olympic Games—with the personal objective of synthesizing a Mexican style that would represent a new epoch for the country: modern, prosperous, and cosmopolitan but aware of its roots. For this project, Legorreta put together a multidisciplinary professional team that allowed him to define that idea of the total artwork in which the architect has the final word.[21] By the 1970s, with proven experience and a design team of his own, he saw the need to design furniture after he received commissions for hotels in Ixtapa, Cancún, and Puerto Vallarta, all for the same chain. He then took up two "traditional" typologies that, by those years, were no longer entirely associated with the colonial—the classic rush chair, or traditional Mexican chair, and the Windsor chair—to design chairs that became furniture lines that complemented the comfort and sense of relaxation that these spaces strove for. The *Vallarta* line (based on the rush chair) and the *Tlaquepaque* line (based on the Windsor chair) showed off Legorreta's design language and became emblematic of his spaces (fig. 18).

In the popular imaginary by the 1970s, the furniture designed by these architects had little to do with recalling the colonial past but embodied a belief that these typologies and references came from "tradition" and "Mexicanness." They both embraced these conditions to make them part of a contemporary style associated with cultural heritage, a local context, and artisanal production, responding to the country's specific conditions and the idiosyncrasies of the time. It's evident that, within this "tradition," the Spanish influence was (and continues to be) present and active but went unmentioned. Instead, it was intentionally blurred into layers of history that made modern Mexico.

By Way of Conclusion

The butaque, the rush chair, and the friar's chair, as well as certain details and decorations previously associated with colonial designs, have become part of national Mexican styles and are disseminated and reproduced as such (fig. 19). To date, many young designers continue to question Mexicanness in design, but some also seek a path toward a Mexican or "Mexicanist" design and, within this paradigm, explore, synthesize, and reinterpret these historical motifs and typologies without really having a clear idea of their origins. Most of these designers understand them as being "traditional" in origin, understood and assumed to be the mestizo condition as it was officialized in the years following the revolution but that was scrutinized and analyzed before it was accepted. It is only recently that the Mexican design field has started to revisit and discuss the class and race implications of the colonial that they have taken for granted, to realize that the Neocolonial was an imposed condition that served to forge a system based largely on cultural appropriation, and to interrogate how it no longer corresponds to present times and beliefs, and—importantly—how to transform it.

Notes

1. For more information on this episode, see Georg Leidenberger, "Las pláticas de los arquitectos de 1933 y el giro racionalista y social en el México posrevolucionario," in *Polémicas intelectuales del México moderno*, eds. Carlos Illades and Georg Leidenberger (Mexico City: Conaculta, UAM-Cuajimalpa, 2008), 188.

2. Here, I refer to Mexico City's Conjunto Urbano Presidente Miguel Alemán (CUPA), finished in 1947.

3. The Estridentista movement rejected conventional religious and traditional values and sought to be a Mexican avant-garde but disagreed with nationalist themes and the propagandistic use that the state was giving the art of the time.

4. Guillermo Sheridan, "Entre la casa y la calle: la polémica de 1932 entre nacionalismo y cosmopolitismo literario," *Cultura e identidad nacional*, ed. Roberto Blancarte (Mexico City: Fondo de Cultura Económica, México, 1994), 384–414.

5. Sylvester Baxter, *Spanish-Colonial Architecture in Mexico* (Boston: J. B. Millet, 1901).

6. Dr. Atl, José R. Benítez, and Manuel Toussaint, *Iglesias de México,* 5, 6 vols. (Mexico City: Secretaría de Hacienda, 1924–27).

7. Federico E. Mariscal, *La patria y la arquitectura nacional: resúmenes de las conferencias en la Casa de la Universidad Popular Mexicana*, 2nd ed. (Mexico City: Impresora del Puente Quebrado, 1970), 12.

8. William Spratling, "El renacimiento de la plata," *Revista de la Universidad de México* 22, no. 11 (July 1968): 12.

9. Daniel Rubín de la Borbolla, *William Spratling: Pionero* (Mexico: Centro Cultural/ Arte Contemporáneo, 1987), 7.

10. In a 1968 article, William Spratling himself stated that his designs had been copied and reproduced *en masse*. Spratling, "El renacimiento de la plata," 9–16.

11. Jorge Rivas Pérez, "Butacas y butaques: sillas nuevas para el Nuevo Mundo," in *Silla mexicana*, ed. Ana Elena Mallet (Mexico City: Arquine, Secretaría de Cultura, 2017), 36.

12. Ibid, 37.

13. Clara Porset, "Folk Furniture of Mexico," *School Arts Magazine* 47, no. 5 (January 1948): 161–67.

14. Rafael Alonso Martínez, "El crecimiento de Marfil Guanajuato, del siglo XVI al XXI," (bachelor's thesis, Universidad de Guanajuato, 2016), http://www.repositorio.ugto.mx/handle/20.500.12059/91.

15. These books were all published by Architectural Book Pub. Co.: *The Mexican House Old and New* (1960), *Mexican Interiors* (1962), *Mexican Homes of Today* (1964), *Decorative Design in Mexican Homes* (1966), and *Houses of Mexico: Origins and Traditions* (1970).

16. Catherine R. Ettinger McEnulty, "Un discurso de modernidad y tradición: Verna Cook Shipway y la representación de la casa mexicana," *Academia XXII* 5, no. 8 (February–July 2014): 75–93.

17. Johanna Lozoya Meckes, "Invención y olvido historiográfico del estilo neocolonial mexicano: reflexiones sobre narrativas arquitectónicas contemporáneas," *Palapa* 2, no. 1 (January–June 2007): 17, https://www.redalyc.org/pdf/948/94820104.pdf.

18. For more on Enrique del Moral and a regional style, see Louise Noelle, *Enrique del Moral: vida y obra* (Mexico City: UNAM-Facultad de Arquitectura, 2004).

19. Claudia Lasso Jiménez, "Antonio Attolini: arquitecto, alquimista, y artesano," *Bitácora Arquitectura*, no. 18 (2008): 16–25.

20. Carlos González Lobo, "La obra de arquitectura de Antonio Attolini Lack," in Ernesto Alva Martínez, Alberto Moreno Guzmán, and Concepción Vargas Sánchez, *Antonio Attolini Lack: arquitecto* (Mexico City: Academia Nacional de Arquitectura, 2009), 11–16.

21. Ricardo Legorreta Vilchis, "Un equipo internacional de diseño," *Arquitectura México* 22, no. 98 (1967): 194–97.

MARINA GARONE GRAVIER

The Neocolonial in the History of Books and Publishing in Postrevolutionary Mexico

The historiography of books and publishing in Mexico holds two distinct positions on the use and function of past graphic traditions. One group correlates the arrival of the typographic printing press in Mexico in the sixteenth century with the beginning of graphic design while the other argues that we can only speak of graphic design after the first half of the twentieth century, particularly as an activity derived from the vitality infused into Mexican publishing by several Spanish exiles, including Vicente Rojo (fig. 1).[1] Both positions rely on the definitions of historical (colonial and nineteenth-century) and modern visuality mainly revolving around the publication of books, magazines, and newspapers. One may chart the arguments correlating the history of local graphic design with the arrival of the book and the printing press and especially with the book as an emblematic element of literary culture.

Well after Mexico's introduction to the printing press, discourses on the histories of books and design began to develop as distinct entities in the late 1950s. The differentiation between graphic products of New Spain and those of the postrevolutionary era was encouraged by a group of people who played a central role in defining culture, education, and the social function of books. Their opinions, interpretations, and comparisons of the colonial past with contemporary, postrevolutionary Mexico are of great importance in addressing the phenomenon of the Neocolonial and its impact on the history of Mexican books and publishing.

Considering these factors, I will analyze some aspects of national identity after the Mexican Revolution to understand, at least partially, the role played by the colonial past in postrevolutionary cultural management. I will then review the work of four individuals who

Fig. 1. Invitation to the exhibition *Vicente Rojo: cuarenta años de diseño gráfico*, Museo de Arte Carrillo Gil, October 17–November 18, 1990. Collection of and courtesy the author.

promoted the colonial typographic legacy as one of the most stable and constant manifestations of national culture through history, namely Joaquín García Icazbalceta (1825–1894), Enrique Fernández Ledesma (1888–1939), Justino Fernández (1904–1972), and Francisco Díaz de León (1897–1975). Finally, I will examine selected texts and publications to understand how the ideas about and the appreciation of past printed materials were shaped and how common ideas about the nature of publishing and the history of the book were conceived in the first half of the twentieth century.

Reading Keys: The Difficult Problem of the Postrevolutionary Definition of National Identity[2]

To at least partly understand the role of the Neocolonial in twentieth-century Mexico, it is necessary to revisit how national identity was received and how past social and cultural structures were recognized. Simply put, the Conquest of Mexico was a watershed that posed a complex process of definition and redefinition of local imaginaries about identity, an identity that has not yet been settled. Part of the oscillating ideological and political solutions included viewing Mexicanness in terms of an "amalgamation," or "hybridization," of Indigenous and Spanish identities.[3]

This same idea of the negotiation of races and languages had already emerged during the colonial period and was perceptible in various literary, pictorial, and artistic manifestations of the time. Although the ideas of mestizo and creole identities were never abandoned, the debates about what it meant to be Mexican were rekindled after national independence in the nineteenth century, which led to differing factions: the localists, including the Indigenists, nationalists, and liberals, and those who emphasized more foreign influences, such as the Iberianists (or prohispanics), imperialists, and conservatives.

The second historical moment of inflection in these debates arose with the Mexican Revolution (1910–20), when the notion of the "hybrid" as consubstantial of Mexicanness was once again taken up. In this context, the cultural projects of José Vasconcelos, the anthropological reflections of Manuel Gamio, and the contributions of philosopher Samuel Ramos, among many other authors, are key to understanding the debates about Mexican identity and psychology. In this essay, I will focus first on Gamio, and then I will consider some of the publishing projects motivated by Vasconcelos's educational crusade.

Already in the final stage of the Mexican Revolution, Gamio suggested solutions to the problem of identity based on the diagnosis that an inherent part of perceived national ills resided in, what he described as, the fusion of races and the convergence of aesthetic, intellectual, and cultural traditions. In the book *Forjando patria* (1916), he proposed linguistic unification, but to the detriment of Native languages. His idealistic perspective was driven by practical purposes: as the inspector general of archaeological monuments and director of the Escuela Internacional de Arqueología y Etnología Americanas (International School of American Archaeology and Ethnology), he proposed the need for a definitive acceptance of the mutual interdependence of Spanish and prehispanic traditions and identities and proposed a route to reach the "new art" that the nation needed. He explained:

The Indigenous class maintains and cultivates the pre-Hispanic art reformed by the Europeans. The middle class keeps and cultivates European art reformed by the pre-Hispanic or Indigenous art . . . we must bring the aesthetic criteria of the former closer to the European-looking art and push the latter towards the Indigenous art. . . . When the middle class and the Indigenous have the same criteria in matters of art, we will be culturally redeemed.[4]

In a way, this discourse was an attempt to push against the use of more autochthonous roots, the neo-prehispanic ones, to define cultural definitions and expectations and to activate neocolonial preferences. However, this spectrum with different accents and manifestations would be the hallmark that would characterize bibliographic projects, publishing, and graphic design of the postrevolutionary era.

The Neocolonial style, which began at the end of Porfirio Díaz's presidency in the early twentieth century, had its peak between 1915 and 1930, although as evident in the writings of Justino Fernández and the magazine *Mexican Art & Life*, later examples exist.[5] This style rejected more current, avant-garde notions of progress, promoted religious values, and carried forward the vertical authority that was common during the colonial era and in the dictatorships of the 1800s. Neocolonial artists and model makers looked to the gothic typefaces and the woodcut frames of the first Mexican prints, blacksmithing, ceramics (tiles and Talavera), and the lapidary inscriptions on colonial buildings. Gothic lettering was more commonly used in advertising than in book design, but there are some examples of it related to the Arts and Crafts movement, such as the covers of the magazine *El Maestro* (December 1921) and the work of F. Orozco Muñoz, *Bélgica en la paz* (1919). Archaizing woodcut frames were also used for the covers of Muñoz's *La Plaza Guardiola* (1942) and Margarita Paz Paredes's *El anhelo plural* (1948), and imitation ironwork was used in *Tres siglos de Arquitectura Colonial* (1933), a publication of the Mexican Department of Education, and Manuel Toussaint's *Guía de Taxco* (1935). The linking of gothic letters and design with allusions to tile forms can be found in Ramón Mena and Nicolás Rangel's *Churubusco-Huitzilopochco* (1921) and José R. Benítez's *Arqueografía de las catedrales de Oaxaca, Morelia y Zacatecas* (1934).

Although the Neocolonial flowered in the 1900s, the appreciation of New Spain's publishing culture started at least around the mid-1800s, when a series of bibliophiles and book collectors began to compile books and documents from the 1500s through the 1700s, with the purpose of forming private and public libraries and making transcriptions and facsimile editions. This Mexican bibliographic movement had close dialogues with peers from other nations, mainly Spain and the United States, who were also interested in incorporating sources from the Indigenous and colonial past of the Americas into the bibliographic movement. The nineteenth century saw the reencountering and reevaluating of part of the Mexican intelligentsia with Novo-Hispanic editions and the construction of the great Mexican bibliographic collections inside of and outside of the country. Joaquín García Icazbalceta would become one of the main architects of colonial book studies. Of his numerous published works, the 1886 text *Bibliografía mexicana del siglo XVI: primera parte, catálogo razonado de libros impresos en México desde 1539 á 1600* is undoubtedly a singular monument in the study of New Spain's printed books.

Ideas & Discussions on New Spain's Publishing History: People, Books, and Magazines

As Rodrigo Martínez Baracs points out, García Icazbalceta's 1855 essay, "Tipografía mexicana," "is the best study done on the difficult topic of the beginnings of printing in Mexico (that is, in the Americas); on the books printed in Mexico, particularly in the sixteenth century, and on the publishers, engravers and lithographers in Mexico; publishing production, gazettes and magazines, bookstores and market conditions during

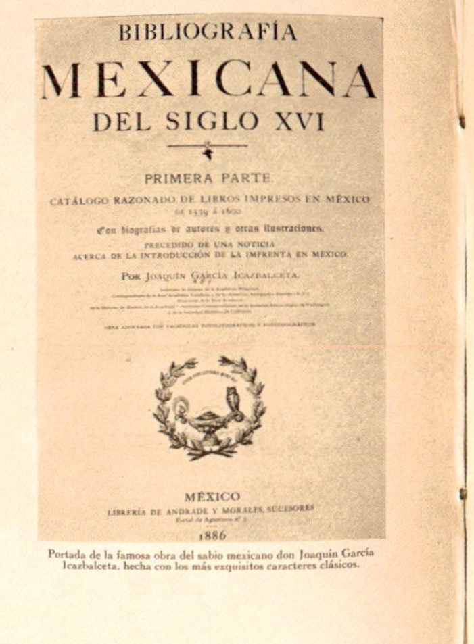

BIBLIOGRAFÍA
MEXICANA
DEL SIGLO XVI
PRIMERA PARTE
MÉXICO
1886

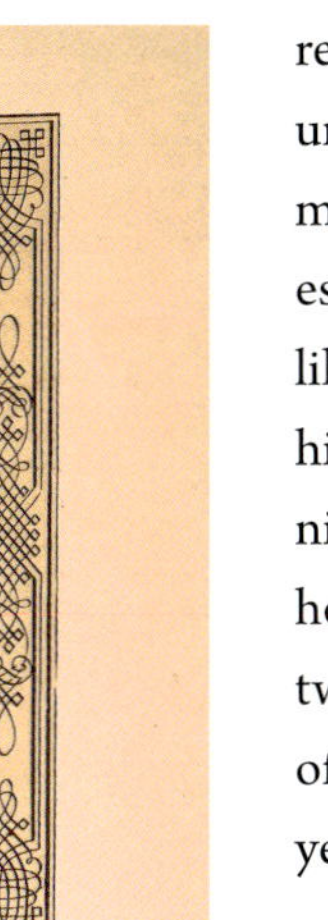

Above: Fig. 2. Enrique Fernández Ledesma, *Historia crítica de la tipografía en la ciudad de México* (1934–35). Collection of and courtesy the author.

Right: Fig. 3. Enrique Fernández Ledesma, *Historia crítica de la tipografía en la ciudad de México* (1934–35). Collection of and courtesy the author.

the colonial period, up to the mid-nineteenth century."[6] Although García Icazbalceta's emphasis was mainly on sixteenth-century printed materials, the author also addressed the most important printers, printed matter, and works, particularly the gazettes and newspapers, of the nineteenth century.[7] Additionally, he gave some history on engraving and commented on the introduction of the lithographic technique in Mexico. Despite the fact that Mexico City was home to twenty-one printing presses, García Icazbalceta analyzed the reasons for the backwardness of the national typographic art, pointing to the high price of (mostly) imported paper, the dependence on foreign typographic materials, low readership, and the fall in general printing prices that impacted typographers' pay. García Icazbalceta argued that low readership imposed a reduction in print runs, which resulted in inflated unit prices, preventing healthy competition with more affordable materials, and he proposed the establishment of a national typography foundry, like the one in Argentina. García Icazbalceta's historical review and his analysis of the state of nineteenth-century Mexican printing impacted how later book production in the first half of the twentieth century would be analyzed by the likes of Enrique Fernández Ledesma almost eighty years later.

Fernández Ledesma was a writer, poet, literary critic, librarian, and academic with an abundant catalogue of poetry, essays, short stories, history, and literary criticism, some of which appeared posthumously. His books, such as *Viajes al siglo XIX: señales y simpatías en la vida de México* (1933) and *Galería de fantasmas: años y sombras del xiglo XIX* (1939), show a scrupulous care and a remarkable beauty, with illustrations by several graphic artists such as Angelina Beloff (1879–1969) and Francisco Díaz de León.[8] He was director and deputy director of the National Library of Mexico (1929–36), where he organized lecture series and numerous commemorative exhibitions. He was responsible for the publication of important cultural works such as Manuel Toussaint's *La litografía en México en el siglo XIX* (1934) and the 1935 facsimile edition of *Los mexicanos pintados por sí mismos* (1855). He also formed the Sección Vigil for librarians, centralizing the works of library science, various cataloging efforts, and bibliology.[9] He put special effort in creating library catalogs of various types of printed materials, including a catalog of pamphlets, a catalog of iconography (vital to researchers, particularly journalists), a catalog of incunabula, and so on.[10]

Historia crítica de la tipografía en la ciudad de México (1934–35) highlights Fernández Ledesma's knowledge of the graphic arts in the Mexican capital, with a detailed account of nineteenth-century printers, and articulates a certain thought and taste about Mexican design (figs. 2 and 3). This work was commissioned by the Fine Arts Department of the Secretariat of Public Education (SEP) in 1935, erroneously celebrating the fourth centennial of the arrival of the printing press in Mexico.[11] Fernández Ledesma commented that this work was made "not to undertake a general critique of 'typographic bibliography,' which would be nonsense, but to organize on typographic grounds the analysis of the most notable and representative Mexican works. This essay aspires to close the enormous gaps, still untouched, that exist about the typographic peculiarities and conditions of our books."[12] Later, he stated that the motivation for the book was "to represent a period of the nineteenth century—a year or a decade—in its typical books, from the exclusively graphic point of view."[13] He explicitly outlined his proposal of analysis based on a canon of literary objects. It is interesting to note that Fernández Ledesma's canon set the standard to draw comparisons to and to discuss advances and setbacks in the art of book-making in Mexico.

A Paper "Agora" for Men of Letters: Three Mexican Magazines (1921–38)

Although it was mainly through books that discussions about publishing priorities and needs circulated, magazines emerged in the post-revolutionary period that sought to put forward nationalistic educational, cultural, and aesthetic ideologies. Among them were *El Maestro: revista de cultura nacional*, *El libro y el pueblo: revista mensual de bibliográfica*, and *Mexican Art & Life*.[14] In these publications, a few key individuals involved with ideas about colonial-era books can be found frequently within their pages.

After the revolution, pedagogically oriented publications gained renewed interest due to the educational and publishing projects of the SEP; thus, *El Maestro* was born, coordinated by José Vasconcelos. Its fourteen issues were published between 1921 and 1923, almost monthly, amounting to about seventy-five thousand copies that circulated in Mexican schools and abroad. A cast of notable artists illustrated the covers and interiors as well as reproductions of colonial and prehispanic motifs.

Like other contemporaneous publications of the same genre, *El Maestro* was intended to offer useful knowledge, with information about the latest educational trends and didactic advances, as well as materials for children, including games, literature, and poetry, and various texts for educators; it was a sort of mini-manual for general culture. But we must not forget that the function and form of the magazine's dissemination, not unlike other neocolonial endeavors, were linked to the concept of "mission," as understood within the context of the colonial period, in which the teacher was seen as a preacher on a holy crusade

Fig. 4. Cover of *El Maestro* 2, no. 3 (December 1921). Collection of and courtesy the author.

against ignorance. To this extent, we see that the attributes of its transportability and its comprehensive, but concise, contents are like those that, in past centuries, were seen in devotional books and primers, books associated with fatherly advice and intellectual guidance (fig. 4).

The year after *El Maestro* was published, *El libro y el pueblo* appeared. It, too, was part of the SEP project that decided which books and magazines would fill the nation's public libraries and that cataloged the written and artistic heritage of the Department of Fine Arts. The magazine's lifespan was not continuous, and the gaps were linked to the various modifications in Mexico's educational trends. Though more modest, like *El Maestro*, it was printed at the Talleres Gráficos de la Nación (TGN). Over time, it included contributions by poet and playwright Xavier Villaurrutia, artists Carlos Mérida and José Julio Rodríguez, illustrators Victaleano León, Felipe Chávez, and Carlos Carrión, photographer Manuel Álvarez Bravo, and in the 1940s, engraver Francisco Díaz de León designed a logo for the publication.

Fig. 5. Gabriel Fernández Ledesma, cover of *Mexican Art & Life*, no. 9 (July 1939). Collection of and courtesy the author.

The magazine *Mexican Art & Life*, under the direction of poet and art critic José Juan Tablada, was published by the Autonomous Department of Press and Publicity (DAPP) and began to circulate in January 1938. It was in English and extensively illustrated, and Díaz de Léon oversaw the typographical layout. An announcement preceding its publication indicated that "the purpose is to make known to the English-speaking public the exponents of our culture, the monuments of past civilizations, the artistic jewels of the colonial era and to provide serious and interesting data on our present life."[15] To achieve this objective, the magazine embraced an attractive graphic presentation. The printing, in color and black-and-white, exemplified the quality that TGN, as one of the key spaces of postrevolutionary Mexican graphic arts production, could produce.

In a review of *Mexican Art & Life*, art historian Justino Fernández pointed out that the overall design of the magazine belonged to the modern graphic movement with a pictorial tendency derived from abstract painting.[16] The covers used reproductions of paintings by Mexican artists or *ex profeso* compositions. Mexican engravings of the twentieth century were also used on the front page and as framing devices that were visually reminiscent of more romantic illustrations for literary works of the 1800s. The visual aesthetic of the publication combined antique and modern graphic elements that mimicked other strategies of defining a national visual identity that combined time periods and cultures.

In July 1939, the seventh issue of *Mexican Art & Life* appeared, dedicated to the celebration of the fourth centennial of the birth of Mexican typography. The publication's cover featured a multichromatic woodcut engraving by Gabriel Fernández Ledesma, brother of Enrique Fernández Ledesma, which reproduced a hypothetical scene of the workshop of Juan Pablos, the first typographer in Mexico (fig. 5). The content was dedicated to a series of texts on the art of the book, in its varied forms and in different historical periods. Rafael García Granados wrote on Mexican precolonial manuscripts. Federico Gómez de Orozco offered a brief chronology of sixteenth-century printing, and Manuel Toussaint spearheaded the review of local printing in the seventeenth and eighteenth centuries. Other historical texts included: "An Early Mexican Xylograph Incunabula" by Edmundo O'Gorman, "Mexican Books in the Nineteenth Century" by Enrique Fernández Ledesma, "Old Mexican Prints" by Gabriel Fernández Ledesma, "Fire Marks & Ex-Libris" by José Juan Tablada, and "Bookbinding in Mexico" by Manuel Romero de Terreros.

It is worth highlighting two additional articles. Ángel Martín Pérez contributed "The Press: A Social and Political School," which according to bookbinder Rodrigo Ortega, "reflects the spirit of the Cardenist era in Mexico, and manifests, perhaps for the first time, the links that should exist for an ethical, responsible and critical press."[17] Martín Perez's ideas about the social aspects of design would have important exponents in the Taller de Gráfica Popular.[18]

The second article, "Outline of Mexican Contemporary Typography," by Justino Fernández, presents a blueprint of how others would come to speak of "design before design."[19] Fernández's article points to the similarities between the political avatars of the early nineteenth century and those from the Mexican Revolution based on the difficulties that the nation's publishing industry experienced at those times. This suggests that when speaking of contemporary typography, Fernández is referring to production during the national reconstruction period. He considers five possible forms of typographic composition:

1. To make a reconstruction of ancient styles, a work rather difficult to do, due to lack of old types and material. 2. To take inspiration in the compositions of bygone days. 3. To confine one's self [sic] to typographic technicalities without aiming at artistic achievements. 4. To attempt free composition with artistic aims, either with constructional tendencies or pictorial intentions (according to the expositions of Attilio Rossi, alter Dr. Modiano) and following modern esthetic methods. 5. To combine what we would call "technical typography"—to distinguish it from "artistic typography"— with the use of artistic elements such as vignettes, cornices, capitals, etc., or simply to search among dry technicalities some effect that would render the composition not only clear and easily legible, but also pleasant, either through a combination of types and spacing of lines or by means of colored inks.[20]

After complaining about an anachronistic style of compositions with neo-prehispanic influence, Fernández assesses "popular typography," considering it a degraded substitute for colonial printing practices, anchored in the decadent taste of the nineteenth century.[21] According to Fernández, the three factors that contributed to advances in book printing were: first-class commercial publishing, private nonprofit publishing, and official publications sponsored by the government and the national university, each contributing to the overall graphic quality and care in editing and design.

In the group of first-class commercial publishers, he cites *Ediciones Porrúa* (1914), *México Moderno* (1919), *Cultura* (1922), and *Cosmos*. And the group of private publishers included: Sociedad de Bibliófilos Mexicanos, Gante Press, Alcancía, Fábula, Barandal, La razón, S.

A., Chápero, Hipocampo, and Arte Mexicano. Finally, within the public sphere, he identifies the Museo Nacional, Talleres Gráficos de la Nación, Departamento Autónomo de Prensa y Publicidad (DAPP), Secretaría de Relaciones Exteriores, Departamento Central del Distrito Federal, the university press for Universidad Nacional Autónoma de México (UNAM), and Fondo de Cultura Económica.

Tellingly, most of the publishers on his list would enter the canon of graphic design in modern Mexico. If, as I mentioned in the biographical sketches, Enrique Fernández Ledesma represents the opinion of a bibliophile on design and typography, Justino Fernández, a central figure in the disciplinary consolidation of art history in Mexico, encapsulates the academic view. He also exemplifies the publisher, since he was also a cofounder, alongside Edmundo O'Gorman, of *Editorial Alcancía* (1932–59), dedicated to publishing "selected works, in limited editions."[22]

In addition to the perspectives of the writer, bibliophile, and art historian, I will add those of a bookmaker and graphic artist to round out the ways in which notions of the antique book came to circulate culturally through the first institution specifically dedicated to the teaching of editorial design in Mexico: the Escuela de Artes del Libro (School of the Art of the Book).

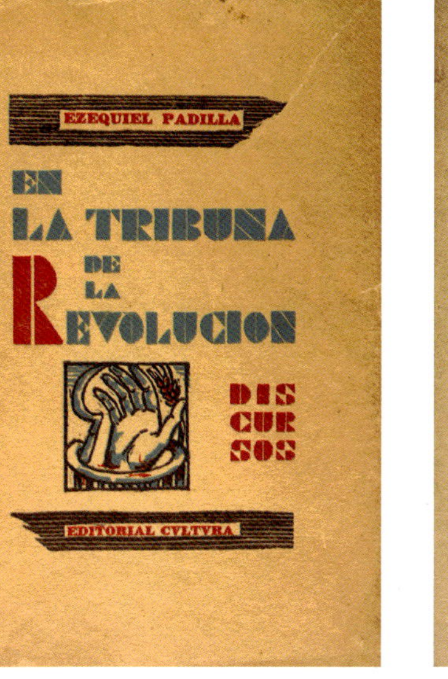

Left: Fig. 6. Ezequiel Padilla, *La tribuna de la revolución. Discursos*, México, 1922, Editorial Cultura, 1929. Cover designed by Francisco Díaz de León. Collection of and courtesy the author.

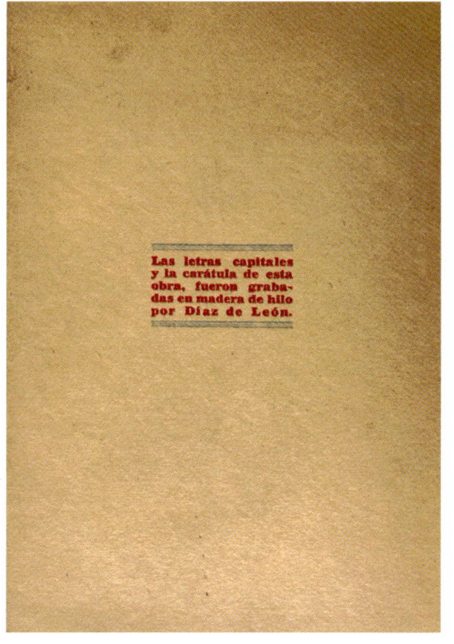

Right: Fig. 7. Ezequiel Padilla, *La tribuna de la revolución. Discursos*, México, 1922, Editorial Cultura, 1929. Back cover designed by Francisco Díaz de León. Collection of and courtesy the author.

Francisco Díaz de León, the Escuela de Artes de Libro, and Its Namesake

Francisco Díaz de León was not only recognized by Fernández Ledesma as a high-level theoretical interlocutor in publishing and typography, but he was also a publisher and typographer himself, that is to say a commentator on and an actor in those trades (figs. 6–8). Díaz de Léon was born in Aguascalientes in 1897, the son of a typographer and bookbinder.[23] From a very young age, he was trained at José Inés Tovilla's Academia de Dibujo (Municipal Academy of Drawing) in his hometown. In 1917, he received a scholarship from the state government to study at the Escuela Nacional de Bellas Artes (National School of Fine Arts), in Mexico City, and the Escuela de Pintura al Aire Libre de Chimalistac (Chimalistac Outdoor Painting School), south of the capital. Between 1920 and 1925, he taught engraving at the Academia de San Carlos (San Carlos Academy), and from 1925 to 1932, he directed the Escuela de Pintura al Aire Libre de Tlalpan (Tlalpan Outdoor Painting School).

His work in publishing dates as far back as 1928.[24] He contributed graphic design for numerous short stories and historical, artistic, and technical essays. His work as a book designer was widely successful between 1930 and 1933 when, together with Gabriel Fernández Ledesma, he was codirector of the Sala de Arte de la Secretaría de Educación Pública (Art Room of the Ministry of Public Education), and also in 1933, he became the director of the Escuela Central de Artes Plásticas (Central School of Plastic Arts) at UNAM. However, his publishing career was made more prominent in 1934 when he was appointed editor of the *Ediciones de Bellas Artes*. He was also art director for *Mexican Art &*

Life between 1937 and 1940 and later, in 1963, the director of the magazine *El libro y el pueblo*.[25]

In 1929, he inaugurated the Artes del Libro workshop at the Escuela Nacional de Artes Plásticas, where he sought to link engraving and *arte editorial* (book design), a combination that he constantly explored in his professional practice. In 1932, he proposed the creation of a school of the art of the book. As Gustavo Adolfo Baz had done in 1882, Díaz de León promoted the creation of a typographic institute to train professionals in the design and manufacture of books, but the project failed to materialize.[26] It was not until 1937 when the SEP inaugurated the Escuela de las Artes del Libro (EAL), under the Department of Workers' Education, and appointed Díaz de León as director that he saw his proposal come to life. The school opened in November 1938, offering six free evening courses for graphic workers and other interested professionals and artists.[27]

In 1943, the school was reorganized around four career tracks: editorial director, engraver, bookbinder, and typographer. It later closed, considered redundant after the creation of the Instituto Nacional de Bellas Artes in 1946. After intense efforts by Díaz de León, it was reopened under the name of Escuela Nacional de Artes del Libro (ENAL), and while five fields of study were originally proposed (publishing director, proofreader, bookbinder, bookseller, and publicist) only three were approved: bookbinding, publishing director, and engraving.[28] In 1958, ENAL became the Escuela Nacional de Artes Gráficas (ENAG) and was located at 117 Bucareli Street, in the Mexican capital.

The school published the magazine *Artes del Libro*, produced entirely by teachers and students, with a few permanent faculty writers, such as Pablo Macías (director of the school and professor of book history), Feliciano Peña Aguilera (professor of ornamental drawing), and José

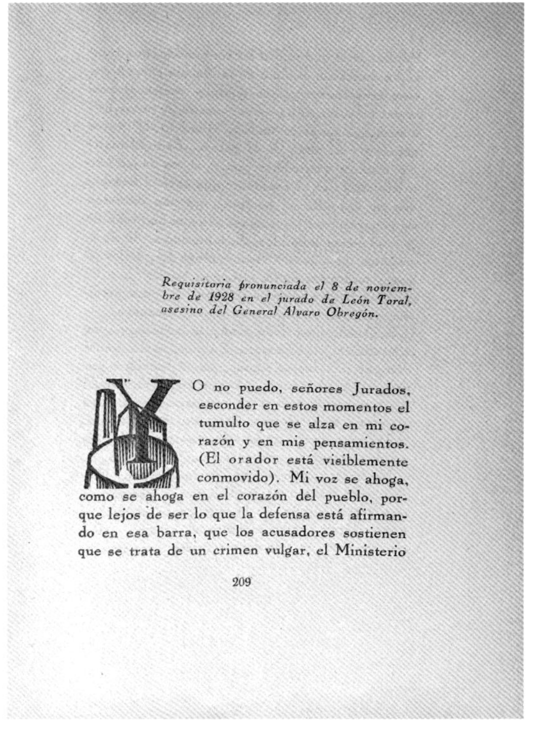

Requisitoria pronunciada el 8 de noviembre de 1928 en el jurado de León Toral, asesino del General Alvaro Obregón.

YO no puedo, señores Jurados, esconder en estos momentos el tumulto que se alza en mi corazón y en mis pensamientos. (El orador está visiblemente conmovido). Mi voz se ahoga, como se ahoga en el corazón del pueblo, porque lejos de ser lo que la defensa está afirmando en esa barra, que los acusadores sostienen que se trata de un crimen vulgar, el Ministerio

209

Fig. 8. Ezequiel Padilla, *La tribuna de la revolución; Discursos*, México, 1922, Editorial Cultura, 1929. Initial page designed by Francisco Díaz de León. Collection of and courtesy the author.

Julio Rodríguez (professor of engraving), who contributed to the ten published issues. Others were more frequent contributors, including Alfonso Tovar Portillo (professor of bookbinding), Antonio Acevedo (editor-in-chief of the publication and professor of proofreading), and Alejandro Stols (UNESCO typography expert at ENAL). Additional collaborators included Pablo Rafael Medina (professor of graphic systems and then of modern illustration systems), Manuel Echauri (professor of publishing), and Amador Lugo Guadarrama (professor of art history), among others. Special mention should be made of Carolina Amor de Fournier, who graduated from the school and then taught the history of the book and French at the institution.[29]

In the third issue of *Artes del Libro*, there are several items that refer to the history of the designer's profession:

Taking advantage of the contribution of a distinguished bibliographer, Dr. Mario Gonzalez Ulloa . . . the

National Museum of Plastic Arts of INBA presented in March of this year the exhibition called "The ancient and modern artistic book in Mexico." Such works were shown as examples of typographic craftsmanship and aesthetics that "make them worthy of conscientious study outside their specific subjects so that book designers, art connoisseurs, and students of specialized schools can find in them secular lessons that affirm or complete their appreciation of the diverse currents of taste with which typographic pages and their illustration have been conceived."[30]

In the same 1957 issue, Stols made some important lexical clarifications when speaking of editorial design and traces the variations that book design has undergone over time.[31] After pointing to an early period when the professions of printer, publisher, and bookseller were united—especially during the period of hand printing—Stols indicated that these professions became more and more separated in the 1800s. The "publisher-printer" for him was represented in individuals such as Aldus Manutius, Robert Estienne, Christophe Plantin and Jan Moretus, the Elzevir family, and Firmin Didot, owners of printing presses who commonly sought their own typographic styles.

Preliminary Conclusions

There is an important discursive continuity between the histories of books and printing and the history of graphic design in Mexico, already well established in the 1930s. In this historical context, the influence of colonial-era books on postrevolutionary typographic design and publishing projects is key to understanding not only the visual and discursive referents of the Neocolonial style but also the definitions and ways of bookmaking promoted in Mexico by those who championed the Neocolonial.

Joaquín García Icazbalceta, Enrique Fernández Ledesma, Justino Fernández , and Francisco **Díaz de León would come to be recognized as critical agents of the history of Mexican design. One branch of this history moves from classical bibliography to design, and the other from the more recent history of books and publishing to graphic design. Once the university began offering a path for careers in design in 1969, a canon could be shared by both disciplines.**

The various opinions about publishing and typographic aesthetics shaped by bibliophiles, art historians, typographers, and art directors were fashioned into a coherent history of Mexican design. A continuity is then observed, and in a certain way, a fusion of colonial publishing history and the Neocolonial is the mortar that bonded a part of the complex Mexican visual identity.

Notes

Parts of this essay first appeared in Spanish in Verónica Devalle and Marina Garone Gravier, eds., *Diseño latinoamericano: diez miradas a una historia en construcción* (Bogota, Colombia: Fundación Universidad de Bogotá Jorge Tadeo Lozano, Ediciones USTA, and Politécnico Grancolombiano, 2020), 21–68. Thank you to Fundación Universidad de Bogotá Jorge Tadeo Lozano for allowing us to include it in this volume.

1. See Vicente Rojo and Pachecho José Emilio, *Vicente Rojo: Diseño Gráfico* (Mexico City: Coordinación de Difusión Cultural UNAM: Consejo Nacional para la Cultura y las Artes Dirección General de Publicaciones: Trama Visual: Ediciones Era, 1996) and Marina Garone Gravier, "Rojo: un camino del diseño a la edicióne," in *Vicente Rojo. Escrito Pintado*, ed. Vicente Rojo and Federico Álvarez (Mexico: Museo Universitario de Arte Contemporáneo, El Colegio Nacional, 2015), 84–134.

2. See Marina Garone Gravier, "Diseño y tipografía que forjaron patria," in *Mexico ilustrado: Libros, revistas, y carteles, 1920-1950*, ed. Salvador Albiñana (Mexico City: Editorial RM, 2010), 54–64.

3. See David Brading, *Los orígenes del nacionalismo mexicano* (Mexico City: Era, 1988) and *Ensayos sobre el México contemporáneo* (Mexico City: FCE, 2020); Agustín Basave Benítez, *México mestizo*, (Mexico City: FCE, 1993, 1992); Natividad González Chong, *Mitos nacionalistas e identidades étnicas. Los intelectuales indígenas y el Estado mexicano* (Mexico City: Universidad Nacional Autónoma de México, 2012); and Guillermo Zermeño, "Del mestizo al mestizaje: arqueología de un concepto," in *El peso de la sangre. Limpios, mestizos y nobles en el mundo hispano*, eds. N. Böetcher, B. Hausberger and M. Hering Torres. (Mexico City: El Colegio de México, 2011) 283–317.

4. Manuel Gamio, *Forjando patria* (Mexico City: Librería de Porrúa Hermanos, 1916), 66. Unless otherwise noted, Spanish quotations translated by Lisbet Barrientos and Kathryn Santner.

5. Garone Gravier, "Diseño y tipografía que forjaron patria," 54–64.

6. **Rodrigo Martínez Baracs, "Joaquín García Icazbalceta y el *Diccionario Universal de Historia y de Geografía*," *Boletín del Instituto de Investigaciones Bibliográficas* 17, nos. 1 and 2 (2012): 9.**

7. **Joaquín Garcia Icazbalceta, "Tipografía mexicana," in *Diccionario Universal de Historia y de Geografía* (Mexico City: Tipografia de Rafael), 961–77.**

8. Ernesto de la Torre Villar, "Francisco Díaz de León," in *Ilustradores de libros. Guión biobibliográfico* (Mexico City: Dirección General de Publicaciones y Fomento Editorial, Universidad Nacional Autónoma de México, 1999), 179–92.

9. Although we do not yet have sufficient evidence to determine when the concept "book design" was first used in Mexico, there is data to inform future research. Biographical articles on Juan B. Iguíniz contain lectures on bibliology given by Alberto María Carreño as early as 1916 in the First National School of Librarians. Alicia Perales de Mercado, "Don Juan B. Iguíniz, el maestro," *Boletín de la Biblioteca Nacional de México*, no. 4 (July–December 1970): 39–43; and Aurora Cano Andaluz and Joel Estudillo García, "Juan Bautista Iguíniz y la historia de la profesión bibliotecaria en México (1915-1971)," *Boletín del IIB* 12, nos. 1 and 2 (2010). Additionally, Segunda Escuela offered courses on the subject. Quotes show Iguíniz himself taught this subject at the School of Librarianship and Archival Studies at the Faculty of Philosophy of the UNAM between 1953 and 1964 (Perales, Ibid. 40).

10. Miguel Ángel Farfán Caudillo, "Bibliografía mexicana e Instituto de Investigaciones Bibliográficas," *Nueva Gaceta Bibliográfica* 17, no. 65 (January/March 2014): 13–40.

11. I say "erroneously" because many attribute the origins of book design in Mexico to Esteban Martin, a printer known to have lived in Mexico in 1535; however, there are no known surviving examples. Remaining historical evidence suggests 1539, when the first typographer in Mexico (Juan Pablos) signed a contract with Juan Cronberger, owner of the Sevillian workshop.

12. Enrique Fernández Ledesma, *Historia crítica de la tipografía en la ciudad de México* (Mexico City: Universidad Nacional Autónoma de México, Instituto de Investigaciones Bibliográficas, 1991), XII.

13. Ibid.

14. Lucía Martínez Moctezuma, "El Maestro. Revista de cultura nacional," in *Revistas culturales latinoamericanas (1920-1960)*, ed. Lydia Elizalde (Mexico City: Conaculta-Universidad Iberoamericana-UAEM, 2008), 15–35; Claudia Escobar and Silvia Salgado, "El libro y el Pueblo, revista de largo aliento," in *Revistas culturales latinoamericanas (1920-1960)*, 35–45.

15. Justino Fernández, "Mexican Art & Life," *Anales del Instituto de Investigaciones Estéticas* 1, no. 3 (1939): 77, http://dx.doi.org/10.22201/iie.18703062e.1939.3.53.

16. Ibid.

17. "Mexican Art & Life No. 7," *Artes del Libro*, accessed April 5, 2024, https://artesdellibro.mx/mexican-art-life-no7.php#:~:text=Angel%20Mart%C3%ADn%20Perez%20refleja%20el,prensa%20%C3%A9tica%2C%20responsable%20y%20cr%C3%ADtica.&text=Romero%20de%20Terreros%20da%-20un,de%20la%20encuadernaci%C3%B3n%20en%20M%C3%A9xico.

18. See Garone Gravier, "Diseño y tipografía que forjaron patria," 54–64.

19. Justino Fernández, "Outline of Mexican Contemporary Typography," *Mexican Art & Life*, no. 7 (July 1939): n.p.

20. Ibid.

21. Ibid. On neo-prehispanic graphic design and its influence on book production, see Garone Gravier, "Diseño y tipografía que forjaron patria," 54–64.

22. Claudia Albarrán, Juan Antonio Rosado, and Angélica Tornero, "Editorial Alcancía," in *Diccionario de literatura mexicana*. Siglo XX, ed. Armando Pereira. 2nd ed. (Mexico City: Universidad Nacional Autónoma de México / Instituto de Investigaciones Filológicas / Centro de Estudios Literarios / Ediciones Coyoacán [Filosofía y Cultura Contemporánea], 2004), 9, http://www.elem.mx/institucion/datos/1504.

23. For a comprehensive biography on Francisco de Díaz de León, see Renata Blaisten, *Francisco Díaz de León* (Barcelona: RM, 2010).

24. He was an illustrator for *Pegaso* y *Forma* and *Diario de Yucatán, Campanitas de plata* (1925), *Día de fiesta* (1938), and *Su primer vuelo* (1945).

25. Claudia Escobar Vallarta, "El Libro y El Pueblo: Índice de Artículos Sobre Bibliotecología y Bibliografía 1922-1926, 1928-1935" (bachelor's thesis, Universidad Nacional Autónoma de México, 2007); María del Rocío García Rey, "La presencia de latinoamerica en las revistas *El Libro y el Pueblo* y *El Maestro*, 1921-1922" (thesis, Universidad Nacional Autónoma de México, 2006); Silvia Mónica Salgado Ruelas, "El Libro y el Pueblo. Revista de largo aliento," in *Revistas culturales latinoamericanas (1920-1960)*, 35–46.

26. Marina Garone Gravier, "Gustavo Adolfo Baz y la idea de un Instituto Tipográfico Mexicano (1882)," *Grafía 10, Cuaderno de trabajo de los profesores de la Facultad de Ciencias Humanas* 10, no. 1 (January–June 2013): 73–89.

27. For the school project, the announcement of the opening, and the first study plan, see Cuauhtémoc Medina, *Diseño antes del diseño: Diseño gráfico en México, 1920-1960* (Mexico City: Museo de Arte Alvar y Carmen T. de Carrillo Gil México, 1991), 97–105.

28. These are promoted on the back cover of issue 1 of the magazine *Artes del libro*.

29. Marina Garone Gravier, "La editora Carolina Amor de Fournier," in *Mujeres hispanas en la tipografía* (Pasadena, CA: Hoffmitz Milken Center for Typography, ArtCenter, 2022).

30. "Noticias y Comentarios: La Escuela de las Artes del Libro anda por ahí," *Artes del Libro* 3 (January–March 1957): n.p.

31. Alejandro Stols, "La tipografía y el libro. Algunos principios," *Artes del Libro* 3 (January–March 1957): 26–28. See also Gabriel Rosenzweig, ed., *Pasión por los libros: Reyes y Stols correspondencia 1932-1959* (Mexico City: El Colegio Nacional, 2011).

Acknowledgments

We express profound gratitude to our esteemed colleagues across the Americas whose generosity and contributions have enriched this volume: Carla García, Marina Garone Gravier, Horacio Ramos, Ricardo Kusunoki Rodríguez, Ana Elena Mallet, and Cristina López Uribe.

Our sincerest gratitude extends to the dedicated team at the Mayer Center for Ancient and Latin American Art, including Lisbet Barrientos, Curatorial Assistant, and Kathryn Santner, Mayer Fellow for Spanish Colonial Art, for their invaluable efforts in organizing the twentieth Mayer Center Symposium.

We also acknowledge the indispensable support provided by the events and audiovisual staff at the Denver Art Museum, particularly Tracey Mattoon-Amos and Stephen Tucker, alongside the security team under the leadership of Lilly Torres. Special appreciation goes to Victoria Lyall, Frederick and Jan Mayer Curator of Art of the Ancient Americas, for her unwavering support and to Christoph Heinrich, Frederick and Jan Mayer Director, for his enthusiastic endorsement of the Mayer Center Symposium series and its ensuing publications.

Gratitude is owed to Nancy Bratton for her exceptional design skills in preparing this publication. We are also indebted to Valerie Hellstein and Leslie Murrell, overseeing publications at the Denver Art Museum, for their expert guidance, editing, and project management. Extensive thanks are further extended to Christina Jackson and her team for their expert assistance with the images.

We acknowledge D & K Printing in Boulder, Colorado, for producing the volume and express our appreciation to the University of Oklahoma Press for its distribution. We extend our special thanks to Natalia Majluf and Kathryn Santner for their generous assistance with translations. Our deepest gratitude is reserved for Lisbet Barrientos, whose meticulous efforts encompassed communication with authors, editing, image procurement, research compilation, proofreading, acquisition of image permissions, and translation for this publication.

On behalf of the Denver Art Museum and the Mayer Center of Ancient and Latin American Art, we convey our profound gratitude to the late Frederick Mayer and his wife, Jan, whose vision and generosity made possible the gathering of distinguished scholars from across the Americas in Denver. The symposium and its accompanying publication stand as enduring testaments to the Mayers' continuing commitment to the fields of Latin and Ancient American art and their enlightened vision to share them with the world.

Jorge F. Rivas Pérez
Frederick and Jan Mayer Curator of Latin American Art
Denver Art Museum

Lynda Klich
Associate Professor
Hunter College, CUNY